I0021411

Internet Wisdom

The Best of Internet E-Mail Wit and Wisdom
by

Greg S. Kessler

Bloomington, IN   Milton Keynes, UK

authorHOUSE™

AuthorHouse™
1663 Liberty Drive, Suite 200
Bloomington, IN 47403
www.authorhouse.com
Phone: 1-800-839-8640

AuthorHouse™ UK Ltd.
500 Avebury Boulevard
Central Milton Keynes, MK9 2BE
www.authorhouse.co.uk
Phone: 08001974150

© 2007 Greg S. Kessler. All rights reserved.

No part of this book may be reproduced, stored in a retrieval system, or transmitted by any means without the written permission of the author.

First published by AuthorHouse 5/2/2007

ISBN: 978-1-4259-3775-1 (sc)

Library of Congress Control Number: 2006904921

Printed in the United States of America
Bloomington, Indiana

This book is printed on acid-free paper.

Dedication

Motivated by my wife, Suzy, inspired by my sons, Beau and Ryan, encouraged by my friends, and determined by my generation, I dedicate this 21st century collection of Internet wit and wisdom.

December 1, 2006
GSK

Table of Contents

Now I Understand
A collection of "Internet E-Mail Wit and Wisdom"

The Internet as we know it today was devised in the United States in the late 1960's by the United States Military to be used as a means to communicate between computers. In 1970 there were very few computers in the world and no personal computers. Since then the computer has evolved exponentially into the single most powerful and amazing electronic device ever conceived. Today the Internet is the way we communicate between people. In a matter of a few short years the collective knowledge, heritage and curiosity of all mankind has been compiled, organized and made available to every person in the world who has access to a computer. This may seem ho-hum to school age kids of the 21st century, but to the vast majority of us living today, this is a mind boggling, overwhelming and daunting phenomenon.

A six year old today has the ability to search the collective knowledge of 6 billion people alive today and the 40 generations of mankind who have compiled history, events, culture and scientific data from all of recorded history.

Even with this awesome tool at hand, the world is still too complex, formidable and mystifying to most of us. Despite the wide-reaching power at our fingertips, most of us merely utilize the Internet to communicate with others. Many of us keep abreast of the events of the day, the fads of tomorrow, or use this incredible device to simply amuse ourselves by playing with the endless diversions and permutations presented by this modern Aladdin's Lamp. Tool or toy, devil or angel, magic lamp or societal menace, today's computer and Internet access is an ever unfolding modern phenomenon. As mesmerizing and tantalizing as the power of the Internet may be, much of the information available is pure brain fodder. Every so often, however, among the limitless explosion of material and matter made available to us through E-mail, there are bits and pieces, kernels of simple lore and homespun wisdom that help us get through the overload of daily life.

The following is but a minuscule outpouring of this trivia and twist. Some of this e-mail wisdom will make you laugh and some of it will make you cry. Some of it will make you think and some of it will make you wonder. For that purpose I commend it to your consideration, judgment, and conscience. In its own way this grassroots *wisdom* says a lot about our world, our culture, our hopes and our dreams. In many ways it breaks down the life force that propels us forward and causes us to understand a little more what life is all about. From the mouths of the anonymous and words of the wise comes a digested and thought provoking look at some of the mystery of today's world. From near and far, past and present, the people of today speak and are heard. Together they speak a common thread of humanity. Maybe the true meaning and power of the Internet is to bring the diversity and common denominators of the world together in a giant meeting place. Speaking and listening together we are coming closer to understanding the path that we all collectively follow. Yes Mr. Gates, we are all connected! *The world is speaking, are we listening?* For your entertainment and enjoyment I present "Internet E-Mail Wit and Wisdom".

Greg S. Kessler
April 1, 2006

"Whatever you do will be insignificant, but it is very important that you do it."

–Mahatma Gandhi

Cost of Raising a Child

The government recently calculated the cost of raising a child from birth to 18 and came up with $160,140.00 for a middle income family. Talk about sticker shock! That doesn't even touch college tuition. But $160,140 isn't so bad if you break it down. It translates into $8,896.66 a year, $741.38 a month, or $171.08 a week. That's a mere $24.24 a day! Just over a dollar an hour. Still, you might think the best financial advise is don't have children if you want to be "rich".

Actually, it is just the opposite.

What do you get for your $160,140.00? Naming rights. First, middle, and last! Glimpses of God every day.

Giggles under the covers every night. More love than your heart can hold. Butterfly kisses and Velcro hugs. Endless wonder over ticks, ants, clouds, and warm cookies. A partner for blowing bubbles, flying kites, building sand castles, and skipping down the sidewalk in the pouring rain.

Someone to laugh yourself silly with, no matter what the boss said or how your stocks performed that day. For $160,140.00 you never have to grow up. You get to finger-paint, carve pumpkins, play hide-and-seek, catch lightening bugs, and never stop believing in Santa Claus.

You have an excuse to keep reading the Adventures of Piglet and Pooh, watching Saturday morning cartoons, going to Disney movies and wishing on stars.

You get to frame rainbows, hearts, and flowers under refrigerator magnets and collect spray painted noodle wreaths for Christmas, and prints set in clay for Mother's Day, and cards with backwards letters for Father's Day. For $160,140.00, there is no greater bang for your buck. You get to be a hero just for retrieving a Frisbee off the garage roof, taking the training wheels off a bike, removing a splinter, filling a wading pool, coaxing a wad of gum out of bangs, and coaching a baseball team that never wins, but always gets treated to ice cream regardless. You get a front row seat to history to witness the first step, first word, first bra, first date, and first time behind the wheel. You get to be immortal. You get another branch added to your family tree, and if you're lucky, a long list of limbs in your obituary called grandchildren and great grandchildren. You get an education in psychology, nursing, criminal justice, communications, and human sexuality that no college can match.

In the eyes of a child, you rank right up there with God. You have all the power to heal a boo-boo, scare away the monsters under the bed, patch a broken heart, police a slumber party, ground them forever, and love them without limits, so…one day they will, like you, love without counting the cost.

What Does Love Mean

A group of professional people posed this question to a group of 4 to 8 year-olds, "What does love mean?" The answers they got were broader and deeper than anyone could have imagined. See what you think:

"When my grandmother got arthritis, she couldn't bend over and paint her toenails anymore. So my grandfather does it for her all the time, even when his hands got arthritis too. That's love." Rebecca- age 8

"When someone loves you, the way they say your name is different. You just know that your name is safe in their mouth." Billy - age 4

"Love is when a girl puts on perfume and a boy puts on shaving cologne and they go out and smell each other." Karl - age 5

"Love is when you go out to eat and give somebody most of your French fries without making them give you any of theirs." Chrissy - age 6

"Love is what makes you smile when you're tired." Terri - age 4

"Love is when my mommy makes coffee for my daddy and she takes a sip before giving it to him, to make sure the taste is OK." Danny - age 7

"Love is when you kiss all the time. Then when you get tired of kissing, you still want to be together and you talk more. My Mommy and Daddy are like that. They look gross when they kiss." Emily - age 8

"Love is what's in the room with you at Christmas if you stop opening presents and listen." Bobby - age 7

"If you want to learn to love better, you should start with a friend who you hate." Nikka - age 6

"Love is when you tell a guy you like his shirt, then he wears it everyday." Noelle - age 7

"Love is like a little old woman and a little old man who are still friends even after they know each other so well." Tommy - age 6

"During my piano recital, I was on a stage and I was scared. I looked at all the people watching me and saw my daddy waving and smiling. He was the only one doing that. I wasn't scared anymore." Cindy - age 8

"My mommy loves me more than anybody . You don't see anyone else kissing me to sleep at night." Clare - age 6

"Love is when Mommy gives Daddy the best piece of chicken." Elaine-age 5

"Love is when Mommy sees Daddy smelly and sweaty and still says he is handsomer than Brad Pitt." Chris - age 7

"Love is when your puppy licks your face even after you left him alone all day." Mary Ann - age 4

"I know my older sister loves me because she gives me all her old clothes and has to go out and buy new ones." Lauren - age 4

"When you love somebody, your eyelashes go up and down and little stars come out of you." Karen - age 7

"You really shouldn't say 'I love you' unless you mean it. But if you mean it, you should say it a lot. People forget." Jessica - age 8

And the final one — Author and lecturer Leo Buscaglia once talked about a contest he was asked to judge. The purpose of the contest was to find the most caring child. The winner was a four year old child whose next door neighbor was an elderly gentleman who had recently lost his wife. Upon seeing the man cry, the little boy went into the old gentleman's yard, climbed onto his lap, and just sat there. When his Mother asked what he had said to the neighbor, the little boy said, "Nothing, I just helped him cry."

Four Lessons

Four lessons to make you think about the way we treat people

1. First Important Lesson - Cleaning Lady. During my second month of college, our professor gave us a pop quiz. I was a conscientious student and had breezed through the questions, until I read the last one: "What is the first name of the woman who cleans the school?" Surely this was some kind of joke. I had seen the cleaning woman several times. She was tall, dark-haired and in her 50s, but how would I know her name? I handed in my paper, leaving the last question blank. Just before class ended, one student asked of the last question would count toward our quiz grade. "Absolutely," said the professor "In your careers you will meet many people. All are significant. They deserve you attention and care, even if all you do is smile and say 'hello'." I have never forgotten that lesson. I also learned her name was Dorothy.

2. Second Important Lesson - Pickup in the Rain. One night at 11:30 pm, an older African American woman was standing on the side of an Alabama highway trying to endure a lashing rainstorm. Her car had broken down and she desperately needed a ride. Soaking wet, she

decided to flag down the next car. A young white man stopped to help her, generally unheard of in those conflict-filled 1960s. The man took her to safety, helped her get assistance and put her in a taxicab. She seemed to be in a big hurry, but wrote down his address and thanked him. Seven days went by and a knock came on the man's door. To his surprise, a giant console color TV was delivered to his home. A special note was attached. It read "Thank you so much for assisting me on the highway the other night. The rain drenched not only my clothes, but also my spirits. Then you came along. Because of you, I was able to make it to my dying husband's bedside just before he passed away. God bless you for helping me and unselfishly serving others." Sincerely, Mrs. Nat King Cole.

3. Third Important Lesson - Always remember those who serve. In the days when an ice cream sundae cost much less, a 10 year-old boy entered a hotel coffee shop and sat at a table. A waitress put a glass of water in front of him. "How much is an ice cream sundae?" he asked. "Fifty cents," replied the waitress. The little boy pulled his hand out of his pocket and studied the coins in it. "Well, how much is a plain dish of ice cream?", he inquired. By now more people were waiting for a table and the waitress was growing impatient. "Thirty-five cents," she brusquely replied. The little boy again counted his coins. "I'll have

the plain ice cream," he said. The waitress brought the ice cream, put the bill on the table and walked away. The boy finished the ice cream, paid the cashier and left. When the waitress came back, she began to cry as she wiped down the table. There, placed neatly beside the empty dish, were two nickels and five pennies.

You see, he couldn't have the sundae, because he had to have enough to leave her a tip.

4. Fourth Important Lesson - Giving When it Counts. Many years ago, when I worked as a volunteer at a hospital, I got to know a little girl named Liz who was suffering from a rare and serious disease. Her only chance of recovery appeared to be a blood transfusion from her 5-year old brother, who had miraculously survived the same disease and had developed the antibodies needed to combat the illness. The doctor explained the situation to the little brother, and asked the little boy if he would be willing to give his blood to his sister. I saw him hesitate for only a moment before taking a deep breath and saying, "Yes, I'll do it if it will save her". As the transfusion progressed he lay in bed next to his sister and smiled, as we all did, seeing the color returning to her cheek. Then his face grew pale and smile faded. He looked up at the doctor and asked with a trembling voice, "Will I start to die right away?" Being young, the little boy had misunderstood the

doctor, he thought he was going to have to give his sister all of his blood in order to save her.

Instructions For Life

1. Take into account that great love and great achievements involve great risk.

2. When you lose, don't lose the lesson.

3. Follow the three R's: Respect for self, respect for others, responsibility for all your actions.

4. Remember that not getting what you want is sometimes a wonderful stroke of luck.

5. Learn the rules so you know how to break them properly.

6. Don't let a little dispute injure a great friendship.

7. When you realize you've made a mistake, take immediate steps to correct it.

8. Spend some time alone every day.

9. Open your arms to change, but don't let go of your values.

10. Remember that silence is sometimes the best answer.

11. Live a good, honorable life. Then when you get older and think back, you'll be able to enjoy it a second time.

12. A loving atmosphere in your home is the foundation of your life.

13. In disagreements with loved ones, deal only with the current situation. Don't bring up the past.

14. Share your knowledge. It's a way to achieve immortality.

15. Be gentle with the earth.

16. Once a year, go someplace you've never been before.

17. Remember the best relationship is one in which your love for each other exceeds your need for each other.

18. Judge your success by what you had to give up in order to get it.

19. Approach love and cooking with reckless abandon.

"The future is much like the present, only longer."

- Dan Quisenberry

Dogs

The reason a dog has so many friends is that he wags his tail instead of his tongue.-Anonymous

Don't accept your dog's admiration as conclusive evidence that you are wonderful.-Ann Landers

If there are no dogs in Heaven, then when I die I want to go where they went.-Will Rogers

There is no psychiatrist in the world like a puppy licking your face.-Ben Williams

A dog is the only thing on earth that loves you more than he loves himself.-Josh Billings

The average dog is a nicer person than the average person.-Andy Rooney

We give dogs time we can spare, space we can spare and love we can spare. And in return, dogs give us their all. It's the best deal man has ever made.-M. Acklam

Dogs love their friends and bite their enemies, quite unlike people, who are incapable of pure love and always have to mix love and hate.-Sigmund Freud

I wonder if other dogs think poodles are members of a weird religious cult.-Rita Rudner

A dog teaches a boy fidelity, perseverance, and to turn around three times before lying down.-Robert Benchley

Anybody who doesn't know what soap tastes like never washed a dog.-Franklin P. Jones

If I have any beliefs about immortality, it is that certain dogs I have known will go to heaven, and very, very, few persons.-James Thurber

If your dog is fat, you aren't getting enough exercise. - Unknown

My dog is worried about the economy because Alpo is up to $3.00 a can. That's almost $21.00 in dog money.-Joe Weinstein

Ever consider what our dogs must think of us? I mean, here we come back from a grocery store with the most amazing haul — chicken, pork, half a cow. They must think we're the greatest hunters on earth!-Anne Tyler

Women and cats will do as they please, and men and dogs should relax and get used to the idea.-Robert A. Heinlein

If you pick up a starving dog and make him prosperous, he will not bite you; that is the principal difference between a dog and a man.-Mark Twain

You can say any foolish thing to a dog, and the dog will give you a look that says, 'Wow, you're right! I never would've thought of that!'-Dave Barry

Dogs are not our whole life, but they make our lives whole.-Roger Caras

If you think dogs can't count, try putting three dog biscuits in your pocket and then give him only two of them.-Phil Pastoret

My goal in life is to be as good of a person my dog already thinks I am.

Trivia Fun...

Many years ago in Scotland, a new game was invented.

It was ruled *"Gentlemen Only - Ladies Forbidden"*....

and thus the word <u>GOLF</u> entered into the English language.

In the 1400's a law was set forth that a man was not allowed to beat his wife with a stick no thicker than his thumb.

Hence we have "the rule of thumb"

The first couple to be shown in bed together on prime time TV were Fred and Wilma Flintstone.

Every day more money is printed for Monopoly than the US Treasury.

Men can read smaller print than women can; women can hear better.

Coca-Cola was originally green.

It is impossible to lick your elbow.

The State with the highest percentage of people who walk to work: Alaska

The percentage of Africa that is wilderness: 28%

The percentage of North America that is wilderness: 38%

The cost of raising a medium-size dog to the age of eleven: $6,400

The average number of people airborne over the US any given hour: 61,000

Intelligent people have more zinc and copper in their hair.

The first novel ever written on a typewriter: Tom Sawyer.

The San Francisco Cable cars are the only mobile National Monuments.

Each king in a deck of playing cards represents a great king from history:
Spades - King David
Hearts - Charlemagne

Clubs -Alexander, the Great
Diamonds - Julius Caesar

111,111,111 x 111,111,111 = 12,345,678,987,654,321

1. While sitting at your desk, lift your right foot off the floor and make clockwise circles.

2. Now, while doing this, draw the number "6" in the air with your right hand. - Your foot <u>will</u> change direction.

If a statue in the park of a person on a horse has both front legs in the air,
the person died in battle.
If the horse has one front leg in the air,
the person died as a result of wounds received in battle.
If the horse has all four legs on the ground,
the person died of natural causes.

Only two people signed the Declaration of Independence on July 4th, John Hancock and Charles Thomson.

Most of the rest signed on August 2, but the last signature wasn't added until 5 years later.

Q. Half of all Americans live within 50 miles of what?

A. Their birthplace

Q. Most boat owners name their boats. What is the most popular boat name requested?

A. Obsession

Q. If you were to spell out numbers, how far would you have to go until you would find the letter "A"?

A. One thousand

Q. What do bulletproof vests, fire escapes, windshield wipers, and laser printers all have in common?

A. All invented by women.

Q. What is the only food that doesn't spoil?

A. Honey (ALL you need to do is boil the bottle if the honey hardens.)

Q. Which day are there more *collect calls* than any other day of the year?

A. Father's Day (Figures!)

In Shakespeare's time, mattresses were secured on bed frames by ropes.

When you pulled on the ropes the mattress tightened, making the bed firmer to sleep on.

Hence the phrase......... "goodnight, sleep tight."

It was the accepted practice in Babylon 4,000 years ago that for a month after the wedding, the bride's father would supply his son-in-law with all the mead he could drink.

Mead is a honey beer and because their calendar was lunar based, this period was called the Honey month, which we know today as the *honeymoon*.

In English pubs, ale is ordered by pints and quarts...

So in old England, when customers got unruly, the bartender would yell at them,

"Mind your pints and quarts, and settle down."

It's where we get the phrase "mind your P's and Q's."

Many years ago in England, pub frequenters had a whistle baked into the rim, or handle, of their ceramic cups. When they needed a refill, they used the whistle to get some service. "Wet your whistle" is the phrase inspired by this practice.

How old is Grandma?

One evening a grandson was talking to his grandmother about current events. The grandson asked his grandmother what she thought about the shootings at schools, the computer age, and just things in general. The Grandma replied, "Well, let me think a minute, I was born before: television, penicillin, polio shots, frozen foods, Xerox, contact lenses, Frisbees and the pill.

There was no: radar, credit cards, laser beams or ball-point pens, Man had not invented: pantyhose, air conditioners, dishwashers, clothes dryers, and the clothes were hung out to dry in the fresh air and man hadn't yet walked on the moon. Your Grandfather and I got married first, . . . <u>and then</u> lived together. Every family had a father and a mother. Until I was 25, I called every man older than me, "Sir". And after I turned 25, I still called policemen and every man with a title, "Sir." We were before gay-rights, computer-dating, dual careers, daycare centers, and group therapy. Our lives were governed by the Ten Commandments, good judgment, and common sense. We were taught to know the difference between right and wrong and to stand up and take responsibility for our actions. Serving your country was a privilege; living in this country was a bigger privilege.

We thought fast food was what people ate during Lent.

Having a meaningful relationship meant getting along with your cousins. Draft dodgers were people who closed their front doors when the evening breeze started. Time-sharing meant time the family spent together in the evenings and weekends-not purchasing condominiums. We never heard of FM radios, tape decks, CDs, electric typewriters, yogurt, or guys wearing earrings. We listened to the Big Bands, Jack Benny, and the President's speeches on our radios. And I don't ever remember any kid blowing his brains out listening to Tommy Dorsey. If you saw anything with 'Made in Japan' on it, it was junk. The term 'making out' referred to how you did on your school exam. Pizza Hut, McDonald's, and instant coffee were unheard of.

We had 5 & 10-cent stores where you could actually buy things for 5 and 10 cents. Ice-cream cones, phone calls, rides on a streetcar, and a Pepsi were all a nickel. And if you didn't want to splurge, you could spend your nickel on enough stamps to mail 1 letter and 2 postcards. You could buy a new Chevy Coupe for $600, ... but who could afford one? Too bad, because gas was 11 cents a gallon. In my day: "grass" was mowed, "coke" was a cold drink, "pot" was something your mother cooked in and "rock music" was your grandmother's lullaby.

"Aids" were helpers in the Principal's office, "chip" meant a piece of wood, "hardware" was found in a hardware store and "software" wasn't even a word. And we were the last generation to actually believe that a lady needed a husband to have a baby. No wonder people call us "old and confused" and say there is a generation gap… and how old do you think I am? I bet you have this old lady in mind…you are in for a shock! **This Woman would be only 58 years old!**

Affairs

The 1st Affair

A married man was having an affair with his secretary. One day they went to her place and made love all afternoon. Exhausted, they fell asleep and woke up at 8 PM. The man hurriedly dressed and told his lover to take his shoes outside and rub them in the grass and dirt. He put on his shoes and drove home.

"Where have you been?" his wife demanded."I can't lie to you," he replied, "I'm having an affair with my secretary. We had sex all afternoon." She looked down at his shoes and said:

"You lying bastard! You've been playing golf!"

The 2nd Affair

A middle-aged couple had two beautiful daughters but always talked about having a son. They decided to try one last time for the son they always wanted. The wife got pregnant and delivered a healthy baby boy. The joyful father rushed to the nursery to see his new son.

He was horrified at the ugliest child he had ever seen.

He told his wife: "There's no way I can be the father of this baby.

Look at the two beautiful daughters I fathered!

Have you been fooling around behind my back?"

The wife smiled sweetly and replied: "Not this time!"

The 3rd Affair

A mortician was working late one night. He examined the body of Mr. Schwartz, about to be cremated, and made a startling discovery.

Schwartz had the largest private part he had ever seen!"I'm sorry Mr. Schwartz," the mortician commented, "I can't allow you to be cremated with such an impressive private part.

It must be saved for posterity. "So, he removed it, stuffed it into his briefcase, and took it home.

I have something to show you won't believe," he said to his wife, opening his briefcase. "My God!" the wife exclaimed, "Schwartz is dead!"

The 4th Affair

A woman was in bed with her lover when she heard her husband opening the front door. "Hurry," she said, "stand in the corner." She rubbed baby oil all over him, then dusted him with talcum powder. "Don't move until I tell you," she said, "pretend you're a statue.""What's this?" the husband inquired as he entered the room."Oh it's a statue," she replied, "the Smiths bought one and I liked it so I got one for us, too." No more was said, not even when they went to bed. Around 2 AM the husband got up, went to the kitchen and returned with a sandwich and a beer. "Here," he said to the statue, have this. I stood like that for two days at the Smiths and nobody offered me a damn thing."

The 5th Affair

A man walked into a café, went to the bar and ordered a beer.

"Certainly, Sir, that'll be one cent." "One Cent?" the man exclaimed.

He glanced at the menu and asked: "How much for a nice juicy steak and a bottle of wine?" "A nickel," the barman replied.

"A nickel?" exclaimed the man. "Where's the guy who owns this place?"

The bartender replied: "Upstairs, with my wife."

The man asked: "What's he doing upstairs with your wife?" The bartender replied: "The same thing I'm doing to his business down here."

The 6th Affair

Jake was dying. His wife sat at the bedside.

He looked up and said weakly: "I have something I must confess." "There's no need to," his wife replied.

"No," he insisted, "I want to die in peace.

I slept with your sister, your best friend, her best friend, and your mother!""I know," she replied, "now just rest and let the poison work."

Life Explained…

On the first day God created the dog. God said, "Sit all day by the door of your house and bark at anyone who comes in or walks past. I will give you a life span of twenty years."

The dog said, "That's too long to be barking. Give me ten years and I'll give you back the other ten." So God agreed.

On the second day God created the monkey. God said, "Entertain people, do monkey tricks, make them laugh. I'll give you a twenty-year life span."

The monkey said, "How boring, monkey tricks for twenty years? I don't think so. Dog gave you back ten, so that's what I'll do too, okay?" And God agreed.

On the third day God created the cow. God said, "You must go to the field with the farmer all day long and suffer under the sun, have calves and give milk to support the farmer. I will give you a life span of sixty years."

The cow said, "That's kind of a tough life you want me to live for sixty years. Let me have twenty and I'll give back the other forty." And God agreed again.

On the forth day God created man. God said, "Eat, sleep, play, marry and enjoy your life. I'll give you twenty years."

Man said, "What? Only twenty years! Tell you what, I'll take my twenty, and the forty the cow gave back and the ten the monkey gave back and the ten the dog gave back, that makes eighty, okay?" "Okay," said God, "You've got a deal."

So that is why the first twenty years we eat, sleep, play, and enjoy ourselves; for the next forty years we slave in the sun to support our family; for the next ten years we do monkey tricks to entertain the grandchildren; and for the last ten years we sit on the front porch and bark at everyone.

Life has now been explained to you.

Women

Facts On Figures: There are 3 billion women who don't look like super models and only eight who do. Did you know Marilyn Monroe wore a size 14? If Barbie was a real woman, she'd have to walk on all FOURS due to her proportions! The average woman weighs 144 pounds, and wears between a size 12-14. One out of every 4 college-aged women has an eating disorder. The Models in the magazines are AIRBRUSHED!!! - NOT Perfect!! A psychological study in 1995 found that 3 minutes spent looking at a Fashion Magazine caused 70% of women to feel depressed, guilty and SHAMEFUL!

Models 20 years ago weighed 8% less than the average Woman. Today they weigh 23% less... Beauty of a Woman ~~ The beauty of a woman is not in the clothes she wears, the figure she carries, or the way she combs her hair. The beauty of a woman must be seen from her eyes, because that is the doorway to her heart, the place where love resides. The beauty of a woman is not in a facial mole, but true beauty in a woman is reflected in her soul. It is the caring that she lovingly gives, the passion that she shows. The beauty of a woman with time, only grows. An English professor wrote the words: "WOMAN WITHOUT HER MAN IS NOTHING" on the blackboard, and directed the students to punctuate it correctly.

The men wrote: "Woman, WITHOUT HER MAN, is nothing." The women wrote: "WOMAN!! WITHOUT HER, man is nothing!"

Our Troops

He's a recent High School graduate; he was probably an average student, pursued some form of sport activities, drives a ten year old jalopy, and has a steady girlfriend that either broke up with him when he left, or swears to be waiting when he returns from half a world away. He listens to rock and roll or hip-hop or rap or jazz or swing and 155 mm howitzzors. He is 10 or 15 pounds lighter now than when he was at home because he is working or fighting from before dawn to well after dusk. He has trouble spelling, thus letter writing is a pain for him, but he can field strip a rifle in 30 seconds and reassemble it in less time in the dark. He can recite to you the nomenclature of a machine gun or grenade launcher and use either one effectively if he must. He digs foxholes and latrines and can apply first aid like a professional. He can march until he is told to stop or stop until he is told to march. He obeys orders instantly and without hesitation, but he is not without spirit or individual dignity. He is self-sufficient. He has two sets of fatigues: he washes one and wears the other. He keeps his canteens full and his feet dry. He sometimes forgets to brush his teeth, but never to clean his rifle. He can cook his own meals, mend his own clothes, and fix his own hurts. If you're thirsty, he'll share his water with you; if you are hungry, his food. He'll even split his ammunition with you in the midst of battle when you run low. He has learned to use his hands like weapons and weapons like they were his hands. He can save your life — or take it, because that is his job. He will often do twice the work of a civilian, draw half the pay and still find ironic humor in it all. He has seen more suffering and death then he should have in his short lifetime. He has stood atop mountains of dead bodies, and helped to create them. He has wept in public and in private, for friends who have fallen in combat and is unashamed. He feels every note of the National Anthem vibrate through his body while at rigid attention, while tempering the burning desire to 'square-away' those around him who haven't bothered to stand, remove their hat, or even stop talking. In an odd twist, day in and day out, far from home, he defends their right to be disrespectful.

Just as did his Father, Grandfather, and Great-grandfather, he is paying the price for our freedom. Beardless or not, he is not a boy. He is the American Fighting Man that has kept this country free for over 200 years...

He has asked nothing in return, except our friendship and understanding. Remember him, always, for he has earned our respect and admiration with his blood. And now we even have woman over there in danger, **doing their part in this tradition of going to War when our nation calls us to do so.**

Sex

"Having sex is like playing bridge. If you don't have a good partner, you'd better have a good hand." Woody Allen

"Bisexuality immediately doubles your chances for a date on Saturday night." Rodney Dangerfield

"There are a number of mechanical devices which increase sexual arousal, particularly in women. Chief among these is the Mercedes-Benz 380SL." Lynn Lavner

"Sex at age 90 is like trying to shoot pool with a rope." Camille Paglia

"Sex is one of the nine reasons for incarnation. The other eight are unimportant." George Burns

"Women might be able to fake orgasms. But men can fake a whole relationship." Sharon Stone

"My mother never saw the irony in calling me a son-of-a-bitch." Jack Nicholson

"Clinton lied. A man might forget where he parks or where he lives, but he never forgets oral sex, no matter how bad it is." Barbara Bush (Former US First Lady, and you didn't think Barbara had a sense of humor)

"Ah, yes, divorce, from the Latin word meaning to rip out a man's genitals through his wallet." Robin Williams

"Women need a reason to have sex. Men just need a place." Billy Crystal

"According to a new survey, women say they feel more comfortable undressing in front of men than they do undressing in front of other women. They say that women are too judgmental, where, of course, men are just grateful." Robert De Niro

"There's a new medical crisis. Doctors are reporting that many men are having allergic reactions to latex condoms. They say they cause severe swelling. So what's the problem?" Dustin Hoffman

"There's very little advice in men's magazines, because men think, 'I know what I'm doing. Just show me somebody naked'." Jerry Seinfeld

"See, the problem is that God gives men a brain and a penis, and only enough blood to run one at a time." Robin Williams

"It's been so long since I've had sex, I've forgotten who ties up whom." Joan Rivers

"Sex is one of the most wholesome, beautiful and natural experiences money can buy." Steve Martin

"You don't appreciate a lot of stuff in school until you get older. Little things like being spanked every day by a middle-aged woman. Stuff you pay good money for in later life." Elmo Phillips

"Bigamy is having one wife too many. Monogamy is the same." Oscar Wilde

"It isn't premarital sex if you have no intention of getting married." George Burns

The Interview With God

I dreamed I had an interview with God.
"So you would like to interview me?" God asked.
"If you have the time", I said.
God smiled. "My time is eternity."
"What questions do you have in mind for me?"
"What surprises you most about humankind?"
God answered…
"That they get bored with childhood,
they rush to grow up, and then
long to be children again."
"That they lose their health to make money…
and then lose their money to restore their health."
"That by thinking anxiously about the future,
they forget the present,
such that they live in neither
the present nor the future."
"That they live as if they will never die,
and die as though they had never lived."
God's hand took mine
and we were silent for a while.
And then I asked…
"As a parent, what are some of life's lessons
you want your children to learn?"

"To learn they cannot make anyone
love them. All they can do
is let themselves be loved."
"To learn that it is not good
to compare themselves to others."
"To learn to forgive
by practicing forgiveness."
"To learn that it only takes a few seconds
to open profound wounds in those they love,
and it can take many years to heal them."
"To learn that a rich person
is not one who has the most,
but is one who needs the least."
"To learn that there are people
who love them dearly,
but simply have not yet learned
how to express or show their feelings."
"To learn that two people can
look at the same thing
and see it differently."
"To learn that it is not enough that they
forgive one another, but they must also forgive
themselves."
"Thank you for your time," I said humbly.
"Is there anything else

you would like your children to know?"
God smiled and said,
"Just know that I am here... always."
-author unknown

Subject: Philosophy

The following is the philosophy of Charles Schultz, the creator of the "Peanuts" comic strip.

1. Name the five wealthiest people in the world.

2. Name the last five Heisman trophy winners.

3. Name the last five winners of the Miss America.

4. Name ten people who have won the Nobel or Pulitzer Prize.

5. Name the last half dozen Academy Award winners for best actor and actress.

6. Name the last decade's worth of World Series winners.

How did you do?

The point is, none of us remember the head liners of yesterday. These are no second-rate achievers. They are the best in their fields. But the applause dies. Awards tarnish. Achievements are forgotten. Accolades and certificates are buried with their owners.

Here's another quiz. See how you do on this one:

1. List a few teachers who aided your journey through school.

2. Name three friends who have helped you through a difficult time.

3. Name five people who have taught you something worthwhile.

4. Think of a few people who have made you feel appreciated and special.

5. Think of five people you enjoy spending time with.

Easier?

The lesson: The people who make a difference in your life are not the ones with the most credentials, the most money, or the most awards. They are the ones that care.

The Super Bowl

A man had 50 yard line tickets for the Super Bowl. As he sits down, a man comes down and asked the man if anyone is sitting in the seat next to him. "No", he said, "the seat is empty". "This is incredible", said the man. "Who in their right mind would have a seat like this for the Super Bowl, the biggest sport event in the world, and not use it?" Somberly, the man says, "Well… the seat actually belongs to me. I was supposed to come here with my wife, but she passed away. This is the first Super Bowl we have not been together since we got married in 1967." "Oh I'm sorry to hear that. That's terrible. But couldn't you find someone else - a friend or relative or even a neighbor to take the seat?" The man shakes his head, "No. They're all at her funeral."

Things You Should Know But Probably Don't

Money isn't made out of paper, it's made out of cotton.

The Declaration of Independence was written on hemp (marijuana) paper.

The dot over the letter i is called a "tittle".

A raisin dropped in a glass of fresh champagne will bounce up and down continuously from the bottom of the glass to the top.

40% of McDonald's profits come from the sales of Happy Meals.

315 entries in Webster's 1996 Dictionary were misspelled.

The 'spot' on 7UP comes from its inventor, who had red eyes. He was albino.

On average, 12 newborns will be given to the wrong parents, daily.

Warren Beatty and Shirley MacLaine are brother and sister.

Chocolate affects a dog's heart and nervous system; a few ounces will kill a small sized dog.

Orcas (killer whales) kill sharks by torpedoing up into the shark's stomach from underneath, causing the shark to explode.

Most lipstick contains fish scales.

Donald Duck comics were banned from Finland because he doesn't wear pants.

Ketchup was sold in the 1830's as medicine.

Upper and lower case letters are named 'upper' and 'lower' because in the time when all original print had to be set in individual letters, the 'upper case' letters were stored in the case on top of the case that stored the smaller, 'lower case' letters.

Leonardo DaVinci could write with one hand and draw with the other at the same time (hence, multi-tasking was invented.)

Because metal was scarce, the Oscars given out during World War II were made of wood.

There are no clocks in Las Vegas gambling casinos.

The name Wendy was made up for the book Peter Pan; there was never a recorded Wendy before!

There are no words in the dictionary that rhyme with: orange, purple, and silver!

Leonardo DaVinci invented scissors. Also, it took him 10 years to paint Mona Lisa's lips.

A tiny amount of liquor on a scorpion will make it instantly go mad and sting itself to death.

The mask used by Michael Myers in the original "Halloween" was a Captain Kirk's mask painted white.

If you have three quarters, four dimes, and four pennies, you have $1.19. You also have the largest amount of money in coins without being able to make change for a dollar.

By raising your legs slowly and lying on your back, you can't sink in quicksand.

The phrase "rule of thumb" is derived from an old English law, which stated that you couldn't beat your wife with anything wider than your thumb.

The first product Motorola started to develop was a record player for automobiles. At that time, the most known player on the market was the Victrola, so they called themselves Motorola.

Celery has negative calories! It takes more calories to eat a piece of celery than the celery has in it to begin with. It's the same with apples!

Chewing gum while peeling onions will keep you from crying!

The glue on Israeli postage stamps is certified kosher.

Guinness Book of Records holds the record for being the book most often stolen from Public Libraries.

Astronauts are not allowed to eat beans before they go into space because passing wind in a space suit damages it.

George Carlin said it best about Martha Stewart ... "Boy, I feel a lot safer now that she's behind bars. O. J. Simpson and Kobe Bryant are still walking around; Osama Bin Laden too, but they take the ONE woman in America willing to cook, clean, and work in the yard, and they haul her fanny off to jail."

This Was Written By a 83 Year Old

Dear Bertha, I'm reading more and dusting less. I'm sitting in the yard and admiring the view without fussing about the weeds in the garden... I'm spending more time with my family and friends and less time working. Whenever possible, life should be a pattern of experiences to savor, not to endure.I'm trying to recognize these moments now and cherish them.I'm not "saving" anything; I use my good china and crystal for every special event such as losing a pound, getting the sink unstopped, or the first Amaryllis blossom. I wear my good blazer to the market. My theory is if I look prosperous, I can shell out $28.49 for one small bag of groceries. I'm not saving my good perfume for special parties, but wearing it for clerks in the hardware store and tellers at the bank."Someday" and "one of these days" are losing their grip on my vocabulary. If it's worth seeing or hearing or doing, I want to see and hear and do it now. I'm not sure what others would've done had they known they wouldn't be here for the tomorrow that we all take for granted. I think they would have called family members and a few close friends. They might have called a few former friends to apologize and mend fences for past squabbles. I like to think they would have gone out for a Chinese dinner or for whatever their favorite food was. I'm guessing; I'll never know. It's those little things left undone that would make me angry if I knew my hours were limited. Angry because I hadn't written certain letters that I intended to write one of these days. Angry and sorry that I didn't tell my family and parents often enough how much I truly love them. I'm trying very hard not to put off, hold back, or save anything that would add laughter and luster to our lives. And every morning when I open my eyes, tell myself that it is special. Every day, every minute, every breath truly is a gift from God. If you received this, it is because someone cares for you. If you're too busy to take the few minutes that it takes right now to forward this, would it be the first time you didn't do the little thing that would make a difference in your relationships? I can tell you it certainly won't be the last. Take a few minutes to send this to a few people you care about, just to let them know that you're thinking of them."People say true friends must always hold hands, but true friends don't need to hold hands because they know the other hand will always be there."I don't believe in Miracles. I rely on them. Life may not be the party we hoped for, but while we are here we might as well dance.

Tomb of the Unknown Soldier

On Jeopardy the other night, the final question was— How many steps does the guard take during his walk across the tomb of the Unknowns ... All three missed it.

1. How many steps does the guard take during his walk across the tomb of the Unknowns and why? 21 steps. It alludes to the twenty-one gun salute, which is the highest honor given any military or foreign dignitary.

2. How long does he hesitate after his about face to begin his return walk and why? 21 seconds for the same reason as answer number 1

3. Why are his gloves wet? His gloves are moistened to prevent his losing his grip on the rifle.

4. Does he carry his rifle on the same shoulder all the time and if not, why not? He carries the rifle on the shoulder away from the tomb. After his march across the path, he executes an about face and moves the rifle to the outside shoulder.

5. How often are the guards changed? Guards are changed every thirty minutes, twenty-four hours a day, 365 days a year.

6. What are the physical traits of the guard limited to? For a person to apply for guard duty at the tomb, he must be between 5' 10" and 6' 2" tall and his waist size cannot exceed 30."

Other requirements of the Guard: They must commit 2 years of life to guard the tomb, live in a barracks under the tomb, and cannot drink any alcohol on or off duty for the rest of their lives. They cannot swear in public for the rest of their lives and cannot disgrace the uniform {fighting} or the tomb in any way. After two years, the guard is given a wreath pin that is worn on their lapel signifying they served as guard of the tomb. There are only 400 presently worn. The guard must obey these rules for the rest of their lives or give up the wreath pin. The shoes are specially made with very thick soles to keep the heat and cold from their feet. There are metal heel plates that extend to the top of the shoe in order to make the loud click as they come to a halt. There are no wrinkles, folds or lint on the uniform. Guards dress for duty in front of a full-length mirror. The first six months of duty a guard cannot talk to anyone, nor watch TV. All off duty time is spent studying the 175 notable people laid to rest in Arlington National Cemetery. A guard must memorize who they are and where they are interred. Among the notables are: President Taft, Joe E. Lewis {the boxer} and Medal of Honor winner Audie Murphy, {the most decorated soldier of WWII} of Hollywood fame. Every guard spends five hours a day getting his uniform ready for guard duty. In 2003 as Hurricane Isabelle was approaching Washington, DC, our US Senate/House took 2 days off with anticipation of the storm. On the ABC evening news, it was reported that because of the dangers from the hurricane, the military members assigned the duty of guarding the Tomb of the Unknown Soldier were given permission to suspend the assignment. They respectfully declined the offer, "No way, Sir!" Soaked to the skin, marching in the pelting rain of a tropical storm, they said that guarding the Tomb was not just an assignment, it was the highest honor that can be afforded to a serviceperson. The tomb has been patrolled continuously, 24/7, since 1930.

How To Make A Woman Happy

It's not difficult to make a woman happy, a man only needs to be:

1. a friend
2. a companion
3. a lover
4. a brother
5. a father
6. a chef
7. an electrician
8. a carpenter
9. a plumber
10. a mechanic
11. a decorator
12. a stylist
13. a sexologist
14. a gynecologist
15. a psychologist
16. a pest exterminator
17. a psychiatrist
18. a healer
19. a good listener

20. an organizer

21. a good father

22. very clean

23. sympathetic

24. athletic

25. warm

26. attentive

27. gallant

28. intelligent

29. funny

30. creative

31. tender

32. strong

33. understanding

34. tolerant

35. prudent

36. ambitious

37. capable

38. courageous

39. determined

40. true

41. dependable

42. passionate

43. compassionate

WITHOUT FORGETTING TO:

44. give her compliments regularly

45. love shopping

46. be honest

47. be rich

48. not stress her out

49. not look at other girls

AND AT THE SAME TIME, YOU MUST ALSO:

50. give her lots of attention, but expect little yourself

51. give her lots of time, especially time for herself

52. give her lots of space, never worrying about where
she goes

IT IS VERY IMPORTANT:

53. Never to forget:

* birthdays

* anniversaries

* appointments she makes

HOW TO MAKE A MAN HAPPY

1. Show up naked

2. Bring something to drink

3. Hand over the remote

To Realize

The value of a sister
Ask someone
Who doesn't have one.
To realize
The value of ten years:
Ask a newly
Divorced couple.
To realize
The value of four years:
Ask a graduate.
To realize
The value of one year:
Ask a student who
Has failed a final exam.
To realize
The value of nine months:
Ask a mother who gave birth to a still born.
To realize
The value of one month:
Ask a mother who has given birth to a premature
baby.
To realize
The value of one week:
Ask an editor of a weekly newspaper.

To realize

The value of one hour:

Ask the lovers who are waiting to meet.

To realize

The value of one minute:

Ask a person

Who has missed the train, bus or plane.

To realize

The value of one-second:

Ask a person

Who has survived an accident.

To realize

The value of one millisecond:

Ask the person who has won a silver medal in the

Olympics.

To realize the value of a friend:

Lose one.

Time waits for no one.

Treasure every moment you have.

You will treasure it even more when

you can share it with someone special.

"Senior" Personal Ads

Some "Senior" personal ads seen in Florida newspapers:

FOXY LADY: Sexy, fashion-conscious blue-haired beauty, 80's, slim, 5'4" (used to be 5'6"), searching for a sharp-looking, sharp-dressing companion. Matching white shoes and belt a plus.

LONG TERM COMMITMENT: Recent widow who has just buried fourth husband, and am looking for someone to round out a six-unit plot. Dizziness, fainting, shortness of breath not a problem.

SERENITY NOW: I am into solitude, long walks, sunrises, the ocean, yoga, and meditation. If you are the silent type, let's get together, take our hearing aids out and enjoy quiet times.

WINNING SMILE: Active grandmother with original teeth seeking a dedicated flosser to share rare steaks, corn on the cob and caramel candy.

BEETLES OR STONES?: I still like to rock, still like to cruise in my Camaro on Saturday nights and still like to play the guitar. If you were a groovy chick, or are now a groovy hen, let's get together and listen to my eight-track tapes.

MEMORIES: I can usually remember Monday through Thursday. If you can remember Friday, Saturday and Sunday, let's put our two heads together.

MINT CONDITION: Male 1932, high mileage, good condition, some hair, many new parts including hip, knee, cornea, valves. Isn't in running condition, but walks well.

"We're all in this alone."

-Lily Tomlin

Strange but True Facts – Part 1

1) Most lipstick contains fish scales

2) In Tokyo, a bicycle is faster than a car for most trips of less than 50 minutes

3) There are 18 different animal shapes in the Animal Crackers cookie zoo

4) Should there be a crash, Prince Charles and Prince William never travel on the same airplane as a precaution

5) Your body is creating and killing 15 million red blood cells per second

6) The king of hearts is the only king without a moustache on a standard playing card

7) There is one slot machine in Las Vegas for every eight inhabitants

8) The Mona Lisa has no eyebrows. It was the fashion in Renaissance Florence to shave them off

9) Every day 20 banks are robbed. The average take is $2,500

10) When glass breaks, the cracks move faster than 3,000 miles per hour. To photograph the event, a camera must shoot at a millionth of a second

11) Tablecloths were originally meant to be served as towels with which dinner guests could wipe their hands

and faces after eating (Some of us still do this today, to the consternation of others)

12) Tourists visiting Iceland should know that tipping at a restaurant is considered an insult

13) One car out of every 230 made was stolen last year

14) If you counted 24 hours a day, it would take 31,688 years to reach one trillion

15) Until the nineteenth century, solid blocks of tea were used as money in Siberia

16) It's illegal to drink beer out of a bucket while you're sitting on a curb in St. Louis

17) The first product to have a bar code was Wrigley's gum

18) A Boeing 747 airliner holds 57,285 gallons of fuel

19) A car uses 1.6 ounces of gas idling for one minute. Half an ounce is used to start the average automobile

What if These People had Jewish Mothers?

Mona Lisa's Jewish Mother: "This you call a smile, after all the money your father and I spent on braces?"

Christopher Columbus' Jewish Mother: "I don't' care what you've discover, you still should have written."

Michelangelo's Jewish Mother: "Why can't you paint on walls like other children? Do you know how hard it is to get that schmutz off the ceiling?

Napoleon's Jewish Mother: "All right, if you're not hiding your report card inside your jacket, take your hands out of there and show me!"

Abraham Lincoln's Jewish Mother: "Again with the hat! Why can't you wear a baseball cap like the other kids?"

George Washington's Jewish Mother: "Next time I catch you throwing money across the Potomac, you can kiss your allowance good-bye!"

Thomas Edison's Jewish Mother: "Of course I'm proud that you invented the electric light bulb. Now turn it off and go to sleep!"

Paul Revere's Jewish Mother: "I don't care where you think you have to go, young man, midnight is long past your bed-time.

Albert Einstein's Jewish Mother: "But it's your senior photograph! Couldn't you have done something with your hair?"

Moses' Jewish Mother: "That's a good story! Now tell me where you've really been for the last forty years.

Bill Clinton's Jewish Mother: "At least Monica was a nice Jewish girl!"

New Elements Added to the Periodic Table

1. Element Name: WOMANIUM

Symbol: WO

Atomic Weight: Don't even go there

Physical Properties: Generally soft and round in form. Boils at nothing and may freeze at any time. Melts if treated properly. Very bitter if not used well.

Chemical Properties: Very active. Highly unstable, Possesses strong affinity with gold, silver, platinum and precious stones. Violent when left alone. Able to absorb great amounts of exotic food. Turns slightly green when placed next to a better specimen.

Usage: Highly ornamental. An extremely good catalyst for dispersion of wealth. Probably the most powerful income reducing agent known.

Caution: Highly explosive in inexperienced hands.

2. Element Name: MANUIM

Symbol: XY

Atomic Weight: 180 +/- 50)

Physical Properties: Solid at room temperature, but gets bent out of shape easily. Fairly dense and sometimes flaky. Difficult to find a pure sample. Due to rust, aging samples are unable to create electricity.

Chemical Properties: Attempts to bond with any WO any chance it can get. Also tends to form strong bonds with itself. Becomes explosive when mixed with KD (Element: CHILDUM) for prolonged periods of time. Neutralize by saturating with alcohol.

Usage: None known. Possibly good methane source. Good samples are able to produce large quantities on command.

Caution: In the absence of WO, this element rapidly decomposes and begins to smell.

I Am Thankful

For the wife who says it's hot dogs tonight, because she's home with me and not out with someone else.

For the husband who is on the sofa being a couch potato, because he is home with me and not out at the bars.

For the teenager who is complaining about doing the dishes, because that means she is at home and not on the streets.

For the taxes I pay, because that means that I am employed.

For the mess to clean after a party, because it means that I have been surrounded by friends.

For the clothes that fit a little too snug, because that means I have enough to eat.

For my shadow that watches me work, because that means I am out in the sunshine.

For a lawn that needs mowing, windows that need cleaning and gutters that need fixing, because that means I have a home.

For all the complaining I hear about the government, because that means that we have freedom of speech.

For the parking spot I find near the far end of the parking lot, because it means I am capable of walking and that I have been blessed with transportation.

For my huge heating bill, because it means I am warm.

For the lady behind me who sings off-key, because it means that I can hear.

For the pile of laundry and ironing, because it means I have clothes to wear.

For weariness and aching muscles at the end of the day, because it means I have been capable of working hard.

For the alarm that goes off early in the morning, because it means that I am alive!

And finally, for too much e-mail, because it means I have friends who are thinking about me.

Observations

The most destructive habit...........................Worry

The greatest joy..Giving

The greatest loss..........................Loss of self-respect

The most satisfying work...................Helping others

The ugliest personality trait........................Selfishness

The most endangered species...........Dedicated leaders

The greatest natural resource....................Our youth

The greatest "shot in the arm"............Encouragement

The greatest problem to overcome......................Fear

The most effective sleeping pill.............Peace of mind

The most crippling failure disease..................Excuses

The most powerful force in life........................... Love

The most dangerous pariah.....................A gossiper

The world's most incredible computer...........The brain

The worst thing to be without.........................Hope

The deadliest weapon............................The tongue

The two most power-filled words................... "I can"

The greatest asset...Faith

The most worthless emotion......................Self-pity

The most beautiful attire............................SMILE!

The most prized possession.......................Integrity

The most powerful channel of communication.....Prayer

The most contagious spirit......................Enthusiasm

Halloween Joke

An extremely modest man was in the hospital for a series of tests, the last of which had left his bodily systems extremely upset.

Upon making several false alarm trips to the bathroom, he decided the latest episode was another and stayed put. He suddenly filled his bed with diarrhea and was embarrassed beyond his ability to remain rational.

In a complete loss of composure he jumped out of bed, gathered up the bed sheets, and threw them out the hospital window.

A drunk was walking by the hospital when the sheets landed on him. He started yelling, cursing, and swinging his arms violently trying to get the unknown things off, and ended up with the soiled sheets in a tangled pile at his feet.

As the drunk stood there, unsteady on his feet, staring down at the sheets, a hospital security guard (barely containing his laughter) who had watched the whole incident walked up and asked, "What the heck is going on here?"

The drunk, still staring down replied: "I think I just beat the shit out of a ghost".

Ya Think?

Joe Smith started the day early having set his alarm clock (MADE IN JAPAN) for 6 a.m.

While his coffeepot (MADE IN CHINA) was perking, he shaved with his electric razor (MADE IN HONG KONG).

He put on a dress shirt (MADE IN SRI LANKA),

designer jeans (MADE IN SINGAPORE), and tennis shoes (MADE IN KOREA).

After cooking his breakfast in his new electric skillet (MADE IN INDIA) he got in his car (MADE IN GERMANY) and continued his search for a good paying AMERICAN JOB.

At the end of yet another discouraging and fruitless day, Joe decided to relax for a while.

He put on his sandals (MADE IN BRAZIL), poured a glass of wine (MADE IN FRANCE) and turned on his TV (MADE IN INDONESIA), and then

wondered why he can't find a good paying job in… AMERICA.

"You can live to be a hundred if you give up all the things that make you want to live to be a hundred."

- Woody Allen

Who was Jesus?

There are 3 good arguments that Jesus could have been Black:

1. He called everyone "brother".

2. He liked Gospel.

3. He couldn't get a fair trial.

There are 3 equally good arguments that Jesus was Jewish:

1. He went into his Father's business.

2. He lived at home until he was 33.

3. He was sure his Mother was a virgin and his mother was sure he was God.

But there are 3 equally good arguments that Jesus could have been Italian:

1. He talked with his hands.

2. He had wine with every meal.

3. He used olive oil.

But there were three equally good arguments that Jesus could have been a Californian:

1. He never cut his hair.

2. He walked barefoot all the time.

3. He started a new religion.

But then there were 3 equally good arguments that Jesus could have been Irish:

1. He never got married.

2. He was always telling stories

3. He loved green pastures.

But the most compelling evidence of all - 3 proofs that Jesus could have been a woman:

1. He fed a crowd at a moment's notice when there was no food.

2. He kept trying to get a message across to a bunch of men who just didn't get it.

3. And even when he was dead, He had to get up because there was more work to do.

Amen.

Golf balls and life...

A professor stood before his Philosophy 101 class and had some items in front of him. When the class began, wordlessly, he picked up a very large and empty mayonnaise jar and proceeded to fill it with golf balls. He then asked the students if the jar was full? They agreed that it was. So the professor then picked up a box of pebbles and poured them into the jar. He shook the jar lightly. The pebbles, of course, rolled into the open areas between the golf balls. He then asked the students again if the jar was full. They agreed it was. The professor picked up a box of sand and poured it into the jar. Of course, the sand filled up everything else. He then asked once more if the jar was full. The students responded with a unanimous — yes. The professor then produced two cans of beer from under the table and proceeded to pour the entire contents into the jar effectively filling the empty space between the sand. The students laughed."Now," said the professor, as the laughter subsided, "I want you to recognize that this jar represents your life. The golf balls are the important things - - your family, your partner, your health, your children, your friends, your favorite passions - - things that if everything else was lost and only they remained, your life would still be full. The pebbles are the other things that matter like your job, your house, your car. The sand is everything else - - the small stuff". "If you put the sand into the jar first, he continued, there is no room for the pebbles or the golf balls. The same goes for your life. If you spend all your time and energy on the small stuff, you will never have room for the things that are important to you. Pay attention to the things that are critical to your happiness. Play with your children. Take time to get medical checkups. Take your partner out dancing.

Play another 18. There will always be time to go to work, clean the house, give a dinner party and fix the disposal." "Take care of the golf balls first - - the things that really matter. Set your priorities. The rest is just sand."One of the students raised her hand and inquired what the beer represented? The professor smiled. "I'm glad you asked. It just goes to show you that no matter how full your life may seem, there's always room for a couple of beers."

"I think that God in creating Man somewhat overestimated his ability."

- Oscar Wilde

If Cars Developed as Fast as Computers

At a recent computer expo, Bill Gates reportedly compared the computer industry with the auto industry and stated: "If GM had kept up with technology like the computer industry has, we would all be driving twenty-five dollar cars that got 1000 miles to the gallon." In response to Bill's comments, General Motors issued a press release stating that if GM had developed technology like Microsoft, we would all be driving cars with the following characteristics:

1. For no reason whatsoever your car would crash twice a day.

2. Every time they repainted the lines on the road you would have to buy a new car.

3. Only one person at a time could use the car, unless you bought "CarNT" or "CarXP." But then you would have to buy more seats.

4. Macintosh would make a car that was powered by the sun, reliable, five times as fast, and twice as easy to drive, but would only run on five per cent of the roads.

5. The oil, water temperature and alternator warning lights would be replaced by a single "general car default" warning light.

6. New seats would force everyone to have the same size butt.

7. The airbag system would say "Are you sure?" before going off.

8. Occasionally for no reason whatsoever, your car would lock you out and refuse to let you in until you simultaneously lifted the door handle, turned the key, and grab hold of the radio antenna.

9. Every time GM introduced a new model car buyers would have to learn how to drive all over again because none of the controls would operate in the same manner as the old car.

10. You'd press the "start" button to shut off the engine.

Moments in Life

There are moments in life when you miss someone so much that you just want to pick them from your dreams and hug them for real! When the door of happiness closes, another opens; but often times we look so long at the closed door that we don't see the one, which has been opened for us. Don't go for looks; they can deceive. Don't go for wealth; even that fades away. Go for someone who makes you smile, because it takes only a smile to make a dark day seem bright. Find the one that makes your heart smile. Dream what you want to dream; go where you want to go; be what you want to be, because you have only one life and one chance to do all the things you want to do. May you have enough happiness to make you sweet, enough trials to make you strong, enough sorrow to keep you human and enough hope to make you happy. The happiest of people don't necessarily have the best of everything; they just make the most of everything that comes along their way.

The brightest future will always be based on a forgotten past; you can't go forward in life until you let go of your past failures and heartaches.

When you were born, you were crying and everyone around you was smiling. Live your life so at the end, you're the one who is smiling and everyone around you is crying.

Tech Support

Dear Tech Support: Last year I upgraded from Boyfriend 5.0 to Husband 1.0 and noticed a slow down in the performance of the flower and jewelry applications that had operated flawlessly under the Boyfriend 5.0 system. In addition, Husband 1.0 un-installed many other valuable programs, such as Romance 9.9, but installed undesirable programs such as NFL 7.4, NBA 3.2, NASCAR 2.4 (which keeps crashing) and NHL 4.1. Conversation 8.0 also no longer runs and Housecleaning 2.6 simply crashes the system. I've tried running Nagging 5.3 to fix these problems, but to no avail. What can I do? Signed, Desperate ***

Dear Desperate, First, keep in mind that Boyfriend 5.0 was an entertainment package, while Husband 1.0 is an operating system. Try to enter the command C:/ I THOUGHT YOU LOVED ME and install Tears 6.2. Husband 1.0 should then automatically run the applications: Guilt 3.3 and Flowers 7.5. But remember, overuse can cause Husband 1.0 to default to such background applications as Grumpy Silence 2.5, Happy Hour 7.0, or Beer 6.1. Please remember that Beer 6.1 is a very bad program that will create Snoring Loudly WAV files. DO NOT install Mother-in-law 1.0 or reinstall another Boyfriend program. These are not supported applications and will crash Husband 1.0. It could also potentially cause Husband 1.0 to default to the program: Girlfriend 9.2, which runs in the background and has been known to introduce potentially serious viruses into the Operating System. In summary, Husband 1.0 is a great program, but it does have a limited memory and can't learn new applications quickly. You might consider buying additional software to enhance his system performance. I personally recommend Hot Food 3.0 and Single Malt Scotch 4.5 combined with such applications as Boob Job 3.6D and that old standby... Lingerie 6.9 (which have both been credited with improved performance of his hardware). Good Luck, Tech Support

Men vs. Women – Let The Games Begin ...

RELATIONSHIPS: When a relationship ends, a woman will cry and pour her heart out to her girlfriends. Then she will write a poem titled 'All Men Are Idiots' and get on with her life. A man has a little more trouble letting go. Six months after the breakup, at 3:00 a.m. on a Saturday night, he will call and say, 'I just called to let you know you ruined my life... I'll never forgive you... I hate you... you're a total floozy... but, I want you to know that there's always a chance for us.'

LOCKER ROOMS: In the locker room men talk about three things: money, football, and women. They exaggerate about money, they don't know football nearly as well as they think they do, and they fabricate stories about their experiences with women.

MATURITY: Women mature much faster than men. Most 17-year old females can function as adults. Most 17-year old males are still trading baseball cards and giving each other wedgies after gym class. This is why high school romances rarely work out.

BATHROOMS: A man has five items in his bathroom - a toothbrush, shaving cream, razor, a bar of Dial soap, and a towel from the Holiday Inn. The average number of items in the typical woman's bathroom is 437. A man wouldn't be able to identify most of the items.

GROCERIES: A woman makes a list of things she needs and then goes out to the store and buys these things. A man waits till the only items left in his fridge are half a lime and a beer. Then he goes grocery shopping. He buys everything that looks good. By the time a man reaches the checkout counter, his cart is packed tighter than the Clampett's car on The Beverly Hillbillies. Of course, this will not stop him from going to the 10-items-or- less lane.

CATS: Women love cats. Men say they love cats, but when women aren't looking, men hiss at them.

OFFSPRING: Ah, children. A woman knows all about her children. She knows about dentist appointments and soccer games and romances and best friends and favorite foods and secret fears and hopes and dreams. A man is vaguely aware of some short people living in the house.

DRESSING UP: A woman will dress up to: go shopping, water the plants, empty the garbage, answer the phone, read a book, get the mail. A man will dress up for weddings and funerals.

LAUNDRY: Women do laundry every couple of days. A man will wear every article of clothing he owns, including his surgical pants that were hip about eight years ago, before he will do his laundry. When he is finally out of clothes, he will wear a dirty sweatshirt inside out, rent a U-Haul and take his mountain of clothes to the Laundromat. Men always expect to meet beautiful women at the Laundromat. This is a myth perpetuated by reruns of old American sitcoms.

MENOPAUSE: When a woman reaches menopause, she goes through a variety of complicated emotional, psychological, and biological changes. The nature and degree of these changes varies with the individual. Menopause in a man provokes a uniform reaction...he buys aviator glasses, a snazzy French cap and leather driving gloves, and goes shopping for a Porsche.

TOYS: Little girls love to play with toys. Then when they reach the age of 11 or 12, they lose interest. Men never grow out of their obsession with toys. As they get older, their toys simply become more expensive and silly and impractical. Examples of men's toys: little miniature TV's, Graphic equalizers, Video games, anything that blinks, beeps, and requires at least six 'D' batteries to operate.

JEWELRY: Women look nice when they wear jewelry. A man can get away with wearing one ring and that's it. Any more than that and he will look like a lounge singer named Ramone.

TIME: When a woman says she'll be ready to go out in five more minutes, she's using the same meaning of time as when a man says the football game just has five minutes left. Neither of them is counting time outs, commercials, or replays.

FRIENDS: Women on a girl's night out talk the whole time. Men on a boy's night out say about twenty words all night, most of which are 'Pass the Doritos' or 'Got any more beer?'

RESTROOMS: Men use restrooms for purely biological reasons. Women use restrooms as social lounges. Men in a restroom will never speak a word to each other. Women who've never met will leave a restroom giggling together like old friends. And never in the history of the world has a man excused himself from a restaurant table by saying, 'Hey, Tom, I was just about to use the "little boys" room. Do you want to join me?'

A Lost Democrat vs. A Lost Republican

A woman in a hot air balloon realized she was lost. She lowered altitude and spotted a man in a boat below. She shouted to him, "Excuse me, can you help me? I promised a friend I would meet him an hour ago, but I don't know where I am.

The man consulted his portable GPS and replied, "You're in a hot air balloon approximately 30 feet above a ground elevation of 2,346 feet above sea level…You are 31 degrees, 14.97 minutes north latitude and 100 degrees, 49.09 minutes west longitude.

She rolled her eyes and said, "you must be a Republican."

"I am," replied the man. "How did you know?"

"Well," answered the balloonist, "everything you told me is technically correct, but I have no idea what to make of your information, and I'm still lost. Frankly, you've not been much help to me."

The man smiled and responded, "You must be a Democrat."

"I am," replied the balloonist. "How did you know?"

"Well," said the man, "you don't know where you are or where you are going. You've risen to where you are due to a large quantity of hot air. You've made a promise that you have no idea how to keep, and you expect ME to solve your problem. You're in EXACTLY the same position you were before we met, but somehow, now it's MY fault."

Subject: Keepers

I grew up in the 40s/50s with practical parents. A mother, God love her, who washed aluminum foil after she cooked in it, then reused it. She was the original recycle queen, before they had a Name for it… A father who was happier getting old shoes fixed than buying new ones. Their marriage was good, their dreams focused. Their best friends lived barely a wave away. I can see them now, Dad in trousers, tee shirt and a hat and Mom in a house dress, lawn mower in one hand, and dish towel in the other. It was the time for fixing things. A curtain rod, the kitchen radio, screen door, the oven door, the hem in a dress. Things we keep. It was a way of life, and sometimes it made me crazy. All that re-fixing, eating, renewing, I wanted just once to be wasteful. Waste meant affluence. Throwing things away meant you knew there would always be more. But then my mother died, and on that clear summer's night, in the warmth of the hospital room, I was struck with the pain of learning that sometimes there isn't any more. Sometimes, what we care about most gets all used up and goes away…never to return. So…while we have it…it's best we love it…and care for it… and fix it when it's broken…and heal it when it's sick. This is true, for marriage and old cars…and children with bad report cards…and dogs with bad hips…and aging parents…and grandparents. We keep them because they are worth it, because we are worth it. Some things we keep. Like a best friend that moved away or a classmate we grew up with. There are just some things that make life important, like people we know who are special…and so, we keep them close! I received this from someone who thinks I am a 'keeper,' so I've sent it to the people I think of in the same way. Now it's your turn to send this to those people that are "keepers" in your life. Good friends are like stars…You don't always see them, but you know they are always there. Keep them close!

TEN THINGS GOD WON'T ASK ON THAT DAY

1...God won't ask what kind of car you drove. He'll ask how many people you drove who didn't have transportation.

2...God won't ask the square footage of your house, He'll ask how many people you welcomed into your home.

3...God won't ask about the clothes you had in your closet, He'll ask how many you helped to clothe.

4...God won't ask what your highest salary was. He'll ask if you compromised your character to obtain it.

5...God won't ask what your job title was. He'll ask if you performed your job to the best of our ability.

6...God won't ask how many friends you had. He'll ask how many people to whom you were a friend.

7...God won't ask in what neighborhood you lived, He'll ask how you treated your neighbors.

8...God won't ask about the color of your skin, He'll ask about the content of your character.

9...God won't ask why it took you so long to seek Salvation. He'll lovingly take you to your mansion in heaven, and not to the gates of Hell.

10...God won't have to ask how many people you forwarded this to, He already knows whether or not you are ashamed to share this information with your friends.

"The best and most beautiful things in the world cannot be seen or even touched. They must be felt with the heart."

-Helen Keller

Mothers II

Somebody said it takes about six weeks to get back to normal after you've had a baby. Somebody doesn't know that once you're a mother, "Normal," is history. Somebody said you learn how to be a mother by instinct. Somebody never took a three-year-old shopping. Somebody said being a mother is boring. Somebody never rode in a car driven by a teenager with a driver's permit. Somebody said if you're a "good" mother, your child will "turn out good." Somebody thinks a child comes with directions and a guarantee. Somebody said "good" mothers never raise their voices. Somebody never came out the back door just in time to see her child hit a golf ball through the neighbor's kitchen window. Somebody said you don't need an education to be a mother. Somebody never helped a fourth grader with her math. Somebody said you can't love the fifth child as much as you love the first. Somebody doesn't have five children. Somebody said a mother can find all the answers to her child-rearing questions in the books. Somebody never had a child stuff beans up his nose or in his ears. Somebody said the hardest part of being a mother is labor and delivery. Somebody never watched her "baby" get on the bus for the first day of kindergarten, or on a plane headed for military "boot camp." Somebody said a mother can do her job with her eyes closed and one hand tied behind her back. Somebody never organized four giggling Brownies to sell cookies. Somebody said a mother can stop worrying after her child gets married. Somebody doesn't know that marriage adds a new son or daughter-in-law to a mother's heartstrings. Somebody said a mother's job is done when her last child leaves home. Somebody never had grandchildren. Somebody said your mother knows you love her, so you don't need to tell her … Somebody isn't a mother.

Puppies For Sale

A farmer had some puppies he needed to sell. He painted a sign advertising the 4 pups. And set about nailing it to a post on the edge of his yard. As he was driving the last nail into the post, he felt a tug on his overalls. He looked down into the eyes of a little boy. "Mister," he said, "I want to buy "one of your puppies." "Well," said the farmer, as he rubbed the sweat off the back of his neck, "These puppies come from fine parents and cost a good deal of money." The boy dropped his head for a moment. Then reaching deep into his pocket, he pulled out a handful of change and held it up to the farmer. "I've got thirty-nine cents. Is that enough to take a look?" "Sure," said the farmer. And with that he let out a whistle. "Here, Dolly!" he called. Out from the doghouse and down the ramp ran Dolly followed by four little balls of fur. The little boy pressed his face against the chain link fence. His eyes danced with delight. As the dogs made their way to the fence, the little boy noticed something else stirring inside the doghouse. Slowly another little ball appeared, this one noticeably smaller. Down the ramp it slid. Then in a some what awkward manner, the little pup began hobbling toward the others, doing its best to catch up..." I want that one," the little boy said, pointing to the runt. The farmer knelt down at the boy's side and said,

"Son, you don't want that puppy. He will never be able to run and play with you like these other dogs would." With that the little boy stepped back from the fence, reached down, and began rolling up one leg of his trousers. In doing so he revealed a steel brace running down both sides of his leg attaching itself to a specially made shoe. Looking back up at the farmer, he said, "You see sir, I don't run too well myself, and he will need someone who understands." With tears in his eyes, the farmer reached down and picked up the little pup...

Holding it carefully he handed it to the little boy. "How much?" asked the little boy. "No charge," answered the farmer,

"There's no charge for love."

* My First and Last Job *

My first job was working in an orange juice factory, but I got canned… couldn't concentrate. Then I worked in the woods as a lumberjack, but I just couldn't hack it, so they gave me the ax. After that I tried to be a tailor, but I just wasn't suited for it. Next I tried working in a muffler factory but that was exhausting. Next was a job in a shoe factory; I tried but I just didn't fit in. I became a professional fisherman, but discovered that I couldn't live on my net income. I managed to get a good job working for a pool maintenance company, but the work was just too draining. So then I got a job in a gymnasium, but they said I wasn't fit for the job. I finally got a job as a historian until I realized there was no future in it. SO I RETIRED, AND I FOUND I AM A PERFECT FIT FOR THE JOB!

What Is A Grandparent?

(taken from papers written by a class of 8-year-olds)

Grandparents are a lady and a man who have no little children of her own. They like other people's. A grandfather is a man grandmother. Grandparents don't have to do anything except be there when we come to see them. They are so old they shouldn't play hard or run. It is good if they drive us to the store and have lots of quarters for us. When they take us for walks, they slow down past things like pretty leaves and caterpillars. They show us and talk to us about the color of the flowers and also why we shouldn't step on "cracks." They don't say, "Hurry up." Usually grandmothers are fat, but not too fat to tie your shoes. They wear glasses and funny underwear. They can take their teeth and gums out. Grandparents don't have to be smart. They have to answer questions like "why isn't God married?" and "How come dogs chase cats?". When they read to us, they don't skip. They don't mind if we ask for the same story over again. Everybody should try to have a grandmother, especially if you don't have television, because they are the only grown ups who like to spend time with us. They know we should have snack-time before bedtime and they say prayers with us every time, and kiss us even when we've acted bad.

A 6 YEAR OLD WAS ASKED WHERE HIS GRANDMA LIVED. "OH," HE SAID,

"SHE LIVES AT THE AIRPORT, AND WHEN WE WANT HER WE JUST GO GET HER.

THEN WHEN WE'RE DONE HAVING HER VISIT, WE TAKE HER BACK TO THE AIRPORT."

Funny Proverbs

A first grade teacher collected well-known proverbs. She gave each child in her class the first half of a proverb and asked them to come up the remainder of the proverb. It's hard to believe there were actually done by first graders. Their insight may surprise you. While reading these keep in mind that these are six-year-olds, because it is really quite amazing.

Better to be safe than...punch a 5th grader. Don't bite the hand that...looks dirty. It's always darkest before...Daylight Savings Time. A miss is as good as a ...Mr. If you lie down with dogs, you'll stink in the morning. Children should be seen and not...spanked or grounded.

If at first you don't succeed...get new batteries. Don't put off till tomorrow what...you put on to go to bed. When the blind lead the blind...get out of the way. An idle mind is...the best way to relax. Laugh and the whole world laughs with you, cry and...you have to blow your nose. Happy is the bride who...gets all the presents. A penny saved is...not much. Two's company, three's...the Musketeers. There are no so blind as...Stevie Wonder. And the favorite:

Better late than...pregnant!

Living in 2006

You know you're living in 2006 when…

1. You accidentally enter your password on the microwave.

2. You haven't played solitaire with real cards in years.

3. You have a list of 15 phone numbers to reach your family of 3.

4. You e-mail the person who works at the desk next to you.

5. Your reason for not staying in touch with friends and family is that they don't have e-mail addresses.

6. You go home after a long day at work and you still answer the phone in a business manner.

7. You make phone calls from home, you accidentally dial "9" to get an outside line.

8. You've sat at the same desk for four years and worked for three different companies.

10. You learn about your redundancy on the 11 o'clock news.

11. Your boss doesn't have the ability to do your job.

12. You pull up in your own driveway and use your cell phone to see if anyone is home.

13. Every commercial on television has a website at the bottom of the screen.

14. Leaving the house without your cell phone, which you didn't have the first 20 or 30 (or 60) years of your life, is now a cause for panic and you turn around to go and get it.

15. You get up in the morning and go on-line before getting your coffee.

16. You start tilting your head sideways to smile. :)

17. You're reading this and nodding and laughing.

18. Even worse, you know exactly to whom you are going to forward this message.

19. You are too busy to notice there was no #9 on this list.

20. You actually scrolled back up to check that there wasn't a#9 on this list.

Bet You Didn't Know. . .

1. Budweiser beer conditions the hair

2. Pam cooking spray will dry finger nail polish

3. Cool whip will condition your hair in 15 minutes

4. Mayonnaise will KILL LICE, it will also condition your hair

5. Elmer's Glue - paint on your face, allow it to dry, peel off and see the dead skin and blackheads

6. Shiny Hair - use brewed Lipton Tea

7. Sunburn - empty a large jar of Nestea into your bath water

8. Minor burn - Colgate or Crest toothpaste

9. Burn your tongue? Put sugar on it!

10. Arthritis? WD-40 Spray and rub in, kill insect stings too

11. Bee stings - meat tenderizer

12. Chigger bite - Preparation H

13. Puffy eyes - Preparation H

14. Paper cut - crazy glue or chap stick (glue is used instead of sutures at most hospitals)

15. Stinky feet - Jell-O!

16. Athletes feet - cornstarch

17. Fungus on toenails or fingernails - Vicks vapor rub

18. Kool aid to clean dishwasher pipes. Just put in the detergent section and run a cycle, it will also clean a toilet.

19. Kool Aid can be used as a dye in paint also Kool Aid in Dannon plain yogurt as a finger paint, your kids will love it and it won't hurt them if they eat it!

20. Peanut butter - will get scratches out of cd's.

Chemistry Mid-Term

Bonus Question: Is Hell exothermic (gives off heat) or endothermic (absorbs heat)?

Most of the students wrote proofs of their beliefs using Boyle's Law (gas cools when it expands and heats when it is compressed) or some variant.

One student, however, wrote the following:

First, we need to know how the mass of Hell is changing in time. So we need to know the rate at which souls are moving into Hell and the rate at which they are leaving. I think that we can safely assume that once a soul gets to Hell, it will not leave. Therefore, no souls are leaving. As for how many souls are entering Hell, let's look at the different religions that exist in the world today. Most of these religions state that if you are not a member of their religion, you will go to Hell. Since there is more than one of these religions and since people do not belong to more than one religion, we can project that all souls go to Hell. With birth and death rates as they are, we can expect the number of souls in Hell to increase exponentially. Now, we look at the rate of change in the volume in Hell because Boyle's Law states that in order for the temperature and pressure in Hell to stay the same, the volume of Hell has to expand proportionally as souls are added. This gives two possibilities:

107

1. If Hell is expanding at a slower rate than the rate at which souls enter Hell, then the temperature and pressure in Hell will increase until all Hell breaks loose.

2. If Hell is expanding at a rate faster than the increase of souls in Hell, then the temperature and pressure will drop until Hell freezes over.

So which is it?

If we accept the postulate given to me by Teresa during my Freshman year that "it will be a cold day in Hell before I sleep with you.", and take into account that I slept with her last night, then number 2 must be true, and thus I am sure that Hell is exothermic and has already frozen over. The corollary of this theory is that since Hell has frozen over, it follows that it is not accepting any more souls and is therefore extinct...leaving only Heaven, thereby proving the existence of a divine being which explains why, last night, Teresa kept shouting "Oh my God."

THIS STUDENT RECEIVED THE ONLY "A"

DICTIONARY FOR DECODING WOMEN'S PERSONAL ADS:

40-ish...49.

Adventurous........................Slept with everyone.

Athletic.................................No breasts.

Average looking................................Moooo.

Beautiful........................Pathological liar.

Emotionally Secure...................On medication.

Feminist..Fat.

Free spirit.................................Junkie.

Friendship first.........................Former slut.

New-Age...............Body hair in the wrong places.

Old-fashioned.............................No BJs.

Open-minded...........................Desperate.

Outgoing..................Loud and Embarrassing.

Professional...............................Bitch.

Voluptuous..........................Very Fat.

Large frame............................Hugely Fat.

Wants Soul mate.......................Stalker.

WOMEN'S ENGLISH:

1. Yes = No

2. No = Yes

3. Maybe = No

4. We need = I want

5. I am sorry = You'll be sorry

6. We need to talk = You're in trouble

7. Sure, go ahead = You better not

8. Do what you want = You will pay for this later

9. I am not upset = Of course, I am upset, you moron!

10. You're certainly attentive tonight = Is sex all you ever think about?

MEN'S ENGLISH:

1. I am hungry = I am hungry

2. I am sleepy = I am sleepy

3. I am tired = I am tired

4. Nice dress = Nice cleavage!

5. I love you = Let's have sex now

6. I am bored = Do you want to have sex?

7. May I have this dance? = I'd like to have sex with you.

8. Can I call you sometime? = I'd like to have sex with you.

9. Do you want to go to a movie? = I'd like to have sex with you.

10. Can I take you out to dinner? = I'd like to have sex with you.

11. I don't think those shoes go with that outfit = I'm gay.

For Attractive Lips

For attractive lips, speak words of kindness.

For lovely eyes, seek only the good in people.

For a slim figure, share your food with the hungry.

For beautiful hair, let a child run his/her fingers through it once a day.

For poise, walk with the knowledge that you never walk alone.

People, even more than things, have to be restored, renewed, revived, reclaimed, and redeemed; never throw out anyone.

Remember, if you ever need a helping hand, you will find one at the end of each of your arms.

As you grow older, you will discover that you have two hands, one for helping yourself, and the other for helping others.

Conspiracy

We Must Stop This Immediately. Have you ever notice that when you're of a certain age, everything seems uphill from where you are? Stairs are steeper. Groceries are heavier. And everything is farther away. Yesterday I walked to the corner and I was dumbfounded to discover how long our street had become. And, you know, people are less considerate now, especially the young ones. They speak in whispers all the time! If you ask them to speak up the just keep repeating themselves, endlessly mouthing the same silent message until they're red in the face! What do they think I am, a lip reader? I also think they are much younger then I was at the same age. On the other hand, people my own age are so much older than I am. I ran into an old friend the other day and she had aged so much that she didn't even recognize me. I got to thinking about the poor dear while I was combing my hair this morning, and in doing so, I glanced at my own reflection… Well, REALLY NOW… Even mirrors are not made the way the used to be! Another thing, everyone drives so fast today! You're risking life and limb if you just happen to pull onto the freeway in front of them. All I can say is, their brakes must wear out awfully fast, the way I see them screech and swerve in my rear view mirror. Clothing manufacturers are less civilized these days. Why else would they start labeling a size 10 or 12 dress as 18 or 20? Do they think that no one notices that these things no longer fit around the waist, hips, thighs and bosom? People who make bathroom scales are pulling the same prank. I actually "believe" the number I see on the dial? HA! I would never let myself weigh that much! Just who do these people think they're fooling. I'd like to call up someone in authority to report what's going on – but the telephone company is in on the conspiracy too; they've printed the phone books in such small type that no one could ever find a number there!

Take Hold of Every Moment

A friend of mine opened his wife's underwear drawer and picked up a silk paper wrapped package: "This, - he said - isn't any ordinary package." He unwrapped the box and stared at both the silk paper and the box. "She got this the first time we went to New York, 8 or 9 years ago. She has never put it on. Was she saving it for a special occasion. Well, I guess this is it. He got near the bed and placed the gift box next to the other clothing he was taking to the funeral home. His wife had just died. He turned to me and said: "Never save something for a special occasion. Every day of your life is a special occasion". I still think those words changed my life. Now I read more and clean less. I sit on the porch without worrying about anything. I spend more time with my family and less time at work.

I understood that life should be a source of experience to be lived up to, not survived through. I no longer keep anything. I use crystal glasses everyday. I'll wear new clothes to the supermarket, if I feel like it. I don't save my special perfume for special occasions, I use it whenever I want to. The words "Someday…" and "One Day…" are fading away from my dictionary. If it's worth seeing, listening to or doing, I want to see, listen or do it now.

I don't know what my friend's wife would have done if she knew she would not be there the next morning. This nobody can tell. I think she might have called her relatives and closest friends. She might call old friends to make peace over past quarrels. I'd like to think she would go out for Chinese, her favorite food. It's these small things that I would regret not doing, if I know my time had come. I would regret it, because I would no longer see the friends I would meet, letter…letters that I wanted to write "One of these days". I would regret and feel sad, because I didn't say to by brothers and sons, not times enough at least, how much I love them.

Now, I try not to delay, postpone or keep anything that could bring laughter and joy to our lives. And, on each morning, I say to myself that this could be a special day. Each day, each hour, each minute is special. If you get this it's because someone cares for you and because, probably, there's someone you care about.

Obituary

It is with the saddest heart that I pass on the following. Please join me in remembering a great icon. The Pillsbury Dough boy died yesterday of a yeast infection and complications from repeated pokes in the belly. He was only 71. Dough boy was buried in a lightly greased coffin. Dozens of celebrities turned out to pay their respects, including Mrs. Butterworth, Hungry Jack, the California Raisins, Betty Crocker, the Hostess Twinkies and Captain Crunch. The grave site was piled high with flours, as long-time friend Aunt Jemima delivered the eulogy, describing Dough boy as a man who never knew how much he was kneaded, Dough boy rose quickly in show business but his later life was filled with turnovers. He was not considered a very smart cookie, wasting much of his dough on half-baked schemes. Despite being a little flaky at times, he even still, as a crusty old man, was considered a roll model for millions. Toward the end it was thought that he would rise again, but alas, he was no tart.

Dough boy is survived by his wife, Play Dough, two children, John Dough and Jane Dough, plus they had one in the oven. He is also survived by his elderly father, Pop Tart. The funeral was held ad 3:50 for about twenty minutes.

More Dog Stuff

If a dog was the teacher you would learn stuff like: When loved ones come home, always run to greet them. Never pass up the opportunity to go for a joyride. Allow the experience of fresh air and the wind in your face to be pure ecstasy. When it's in your best interest, practice obedience. Let others know when they've invaded your territory. Take naps. Stretch before rising. Run, romp, and play daily. Thrive on attention and let people touch you. Avoid biting when a simple growl will do. On warm days, stop to lie on your back on the grass. On hot days, drink lots of water and lie under a shady tree. When you're happy, dance around and wag your entire body. No matter how often you're scolded, don't buy into the guilt thing and pout, run right back and make friends. Delight in the simple joy of a long walk. Eat with gusto and enthusiasm. Stop when you have had enough. Be loyal. Never pretend to be something you're not. If what you want lies buried, dig until you find it. When someone is having a bad day, be silent, sit close by and nuzzle them gently.

Marriage

1. Marriage is not a word. It's a sentence (a life sentence).

2. Marriage is love. Love is blind. Therefore marriage is an institution for the blind.

3. Marriage is an institution in which a man loses his Bachelor's Degree and the woman gets her Masters.

4. Marriage is a three ring circus: engagement ring, wedding ring and Suffering.

5. Married life is full of excitement and frustration: In the first year of marriage, the man speaks and the woman listens. In the second year, the woman speaks and the man listens. In the third year, they both speak and the NEIGHBORS listen.

6. Getting married is very much like going to a restaurant with friends. You order what you want, and when you see what the other person has, you wish you had ordered that instead.

7. There was this man who muttered a few words in the church and found himself married. A year later he muttered something in his sleep and found himself divorced.

8. A happy marriage is a matter of giving and taking; the husband gives and the wife takes.

9.   Son: How much does it cost to get married, Dad? Father: I don't know son, I'm still paying for it.

10. Son: Is it true Dad? I heard that in ancient China, a man doesn't know his wife until he marries her. Father: That happens everywhere, son, EVERYWHERE!

11. Love is one long sweet dream, and marriage is the alarm clock.

12. They say that when a man holds a woman's hand before marriage, it is love; after marriage it is self-defense.

13. When a newly married man looks happy, we know why. But when a 10-year married man looks happy, we wonder why.

14. There was this lover who said that he would go through hell for her. They got married, and now he is going through HELL.

15. Confucius says: man who sinks into woman's arm soon have arms in woman's sink.

16. When a man steals your wife, there is no better revenge than to let him keep her.

17. Eighty percent of married man cheat in America, the rest cheat in Europe.

18. After marriage, husband and wife become two sides of a coin. They just can't face each other, but still they stay together.

19. Marriage is man and a woman become one. The trouble starts when they try to decide which one.

20. Before marriage, a man yearns for the woman he loves. After the marriage the "Y" becomes silent.

21. I married Miss Right, I just didn't know her first name was Always .

22. It's not true that married men live longer than single men, it only seems longer.

23. Losing a wife can be hard. In my case, it was almost impossible.

24. A man was complaining to a friend: I HAD IT ALL-MONEY, A BEAUTIFUL HOUSE, THE LOVE OF A BEAUTIFUL WOMAN, THEN POW! IT WAS ALL GONE. WHAT HAPPENED, asked his friend. He says MY WIFE FOUND OUT.

25. WIFE: Let's go out and have some fun tonight. HUSBAND: OK, but if you get home before I do, leave the hallway lights on.

26. At a cocktail party, one woman said to another: AREN'T YOU WEARING YOUR RING ON THE WRONG FINGER? The other replied, YES, I, AM. I MARRIED THE WRONG MAN.

27. Man is incomplete until he gets married, then he is finished.

28. It doesn't matter how often a married man changes his job, he still ends up with the same boss.

29. A man inserted an ad in the paper - WIFE WANTED. The next day he received a hundred letters and they all said the same thing - YOU CAN HAVE MINE.

30. When a man opens the door of his car for his wife, you can be sure of one thing - either the car is new or the wife is.

Oxymorons

1. Is it good if a vacuum really sucks?

2. Why is the third hand on the watch called the second hand?

3. If a word is misspelled in the dictionary, how would we ever know?

4. If Webster wrote the first dictionary, where did he find the words?

5. Why do we say something is out of whack? What is a whack?

6. Why do "slow down" and "slow up" mean the same thing?

7. Why do "fat chance" and "slim chance" mean the same thing?

8. Why do "tug" boats push their barges?

9. Why do we sing "Take me out to the ball game" when we are already there?

10. Why are they called "stands" when they are made for sitting?

11. Why is it called "after dark" when it really is "after light"?

12. Doesn't "expecting the unexpected" make the unexpected expected?

13. Why are a "wise man" and a "wise guy" opposites?

14. Why do "overlook" and "oversee" mean opposite things?

15. Why is "phonics" not spelled the way it sounds?

16. If work is so terrific, why do they have to pay you to do it?

17. If all the world is a stage, where is the audience sitting?

18. If love is blind, why is lingerie so popular?

19. If you are cross-eyed and have dyslexia, can you read all right?

20. Why is bra singular and panties plural?

21. Why do you press harder on the buttons of a remote control when you know the batteries are dead?

22. Why do we put suits in garment bags and garments in a suitcase?

23. How come abbreviated is such a long word?

24. Why do we wash bath towels? Aren't we clean when we use them?

25. Why doesn't glue stick to the inside of the bottle?

26. Why do they call it a TV set when you only have one?

27. Christmas oxymoron: What other time of the year do you sit in front of a dead tree and eat candy out of your socks?

THE POSITIVE SIDE OF LIFE

Living on Earth is expensive, but it does include a free trip around the sun every year.

How long a minute is depends on what side of the bathroom door you're on. Birth dates are good for you; the more you have, the longer you live. Happiness comes through doors you didn't even know you left open. Ever notice that the people who are late are often much jollier than the people who have to wait for them? Most of us go to our grave with our music still inside of us. If Wal-Mart is lowering prices every day, how come nothing is free yet?

You may be only one person in the world, but you may also be the world to one person. Some mistakes are too much fun to only make once. Don't cry because it's over; smile because it happened.

We could learn a lot from crayons: some are sharp, some are pretty, some are dull, some have weird names, and all are different colors…but they all exist very nicely in the same box.

A truly happy person is one who can enjoy the scenery on a detour.

Heaven...

The couple were eight-five years old, and had been married for sixty years. Though they were far from rich, they managed to get by because they watched their pennies. Though not young, they were in very good health, largely due to the wife's insistence on healthy foods and exercise for the last decade. One day, their good health didn't help when they went on a rare vacation and their plane crashed, sending them off to Heaven.

They reached the pearly gates and St. Peter escorted them inside. He took them to a beautiful mansion, furnished in gold and fine silks, with a fully stocked kitchen and a waterfall in the master bath. A maid could be seen hanging their favorite clothes in the closet. They gasped when he said, "Welcome to Heaven. This will be your home now." The old man asked Peter how much all this was going to cost. "Why, nothing," Peter replied, "remember, this is your reward in Heaven."

The old man looked out the window and right there he saw a championship golf course, finer and more beautiful than any ever-build on Earth. "What are the greens fees?" grumbled the old man. "This is Heaven, "St Peter replied. "You can play for free, every day."

Next they went to the clubhouse and saw the lavish buffet lunch, with every imaginable cuisine laid out before them, from seafood to steaks to exotic deserts, free flowing beverages. "Don't even ask," St. Peter said to the man. "This is Heaven, it is all free for you to enjoy."

The old man looked around and glanced at his nervously at his wife. "Well, where are the low fat and low cholesterol foods and the decaffeinated tea?" He asked. "That's the best part," said St. Peter to the man. "You can eat and drink as much as you like of whatever you like, and you will never get fat or sick. This is Heaven!"

The old man pushed, "No gym to work out at?"

"Not unless you want to," was the answer.

No testing my sugar or blood pressure or…"

"Never again. All you do is enjoy yourself."

The old man glared at his wife and said, "You and your frigging bran muffins. We could have been here ten years ago!"

"Love is not blind - it sees more, not less. But because it sees, more, it is willing to see less."

- Rabbi Julius Gordon

"Not only is the universe stranger that we imagine, it is stranger than we can imagine."

- Sir Arthur Eddington

"The second half of a man's life is made up of nothing but the habits he as acquired during the first half."

- Fyodor Dostoevsky

"He's turned his life around. He used to be depressed and miserable. Now he is miserable and depressed."

- David Frost

"Don't go through life, GROW through life."

- Eric Butterworth

How To Speak About Women And Be Politically Correct

1. She is not a BABE or a CHICK - She is a BREASTED AMERICAN.

2. She is not a SCREAMER or MOANER - She is VOCALLY APPRECIATIVE.

3. She is not EASY - She is HORIZONTALLY ACCESSIBLE.

4. She is not DUMB - She is a DETOUR OFF THE INFORMATION SUPERHIGHWAY.

5. She has not BEEN AROUND - She is a PREVIOUSLY ENJOYED COMPANION.

6. She is not an AIRHEAD - She is REALITY IMPAIRED.

7. She does not get DRUNK or TIPSY - She gets CHEMICALLY INCONVENIENCED.

8. She does not have BREAST IMPLANTS - She is SURGICALLY ENHANCED.

9. She does not NAG YOU - She becomes VERBALLY REPETITIVE.

10. She is not a SLUT - She is SEXUALLY EXTR-OVERTED.

11. She does not have MAJOR LEAGUE HOOTERS - She is PECTORALLY SUPERIOR.

12. She is not a TWO-BIT WHORE - She is a LOW COST PROVIDER.

How To Speak About Men And Be Politically Correct

1.   He does not have a BEER GUT - He has developed a GRAIN ALCOHOL STORAGE FACILITY.

2.   He is not a BAD DANCER - He is OVERLY CAUCASIAN.

3.   He does not GET LOST ALL THE TIME - He INVESTIGATES ALTERNATIVE DESTINATIONS.

4.   He is not BALDING - He is in FOLLICLE REGRESSION.

5.   He is not a CRADLE ROBBER - He prefers GENERATIONALLY DIFFERENTIAL RELATIONSHIPS.

6.   He does not get FALLING-DOWN DRUNK - He becomes ACCIDENTALLY HORIZONTAL.

7.   He does not act like a TOTAL ASS - He develops a case of RECTAL-CRANIAL INVERSION.

8.   He is not a MALE CHAUVINIST PIG - He has SWINE EMPATHY.

9.   He is not afraid of COMMITMENT - He is MONOGAMOUSLY CHALLENGED

10. He is not HORNY - He is SEXUALLY FOCUSED.

IF I KNEW

If I knew it would be the last time that I'd see you fall asleep, I would tuck you in more tightly and pray the Lord, your soul to keep. If I knew it would be the last time that I see you walk out the door, I would give you a hug and kiss and call you back for one more. If I knew it would be the last time I'd hear your voice lifted up in praise, I would video tape each action and word, so I could play them back day after day. If I knew it would be the last time, I could spare an extra minute to stop and say "I love you," instead of assuming you would KNOW I do. If I knew it would be the last time I would be there to share your day, Well I'm sure you'll have so many more, so I can let just this one slip away. For surely there's always tomorrow to make up for an oversight, and we always get a second chance to make everything just right. There will always be another day to say "I love you," And certainly there's another chance to say our "Anything I can do?" But just in case I might be wrong, and today is all I get, I'd like to say how much I love you and I hope we never forget. Tomorrow is not promised to anyone, young or old alike, And today may be the last chance you get to hold your loved one tight. So if you're waiting for tomorrow, why not do it today? For if tomorrow never comes, you'll surely regret the day, that you didn't take that extra time for a smile, a hug, or a kiss and you were too busy to grant someone, what turned out to be their one last wish. So hold your loved ones close today, and whisper in their ear, Tell them how much you love them and that you'll always hold them dear. Take time to say "I'm sorry," "Please forgive me," "Thank you," or "It's okay." And if tomorrow never comes, you'll have no regrets about today.

Stress Management

A lecturer, when explaining stress management to an audience, raised a glass of water and asked, "how heavy is this glass of water?" Answers called outranged from 20g to 500g. The lecturer replied, "The absolute weight doesn't matter. It depends on how long you try to hold it." If I hold it for a minute, that's not a problem. If I hold it for an hour, I'll have an ache in my right arm. If I hold it for a day, you'll have to call an ambulance. In each case, it's the same weight, but the longer I hold it, the heavier it becomes."He continued, "And that's the way it is with stress management. If we carry our burdens all the time, sooner or later, as the burden becomes increasingly heavy, we won't be able to carry on. As with the glass of water, you have to put it down for a while and rest before holding it again. When we're refreshed, we can carry on with the burden.""So, before you return home tonight, put the burden of work down. Don't carry it home. You can pick it up tomorrow. Whatever burdens you're carrying now, let them down for a moment if you can." "Relax; pick them up later after you've rested. Life is short. Enjoy it! And then he shared some ways of dealing with the burdens of life: Accept that some days you're the pigeon, and some days you're the statue. Always keep your words soft and sweet, just in case you have to eat them. Always read stuff that will make you look good if you die in the middle of it. Drive carefully. It's not only cars that can be recalled by their maker. If you can't be kind, at least have the decency to be vague. If you lend someone $20 and never see that person again, it was probably worth it. Never buy a car you can't push. Nobody cares if you can't dance well. Just get up and dance. When everything's coming your way, you're in the wrong lane. Birthdays are good for you. The more you have, the longer you live.

A Wonderful Message by George Carlin

The paradox of our time in history is that we have taller buildings but shorter tempers, wider freeways, but narrower viewpoints. We spend more, but have less, we buy more, but enjoy less.

We have bigger houses and smaller families, more conveniences, but less time. We have more degrees but less sense, more knowledge, but less judgment, more experts, yet more problems, more medicine, but less wellness. We drink too much, smoke too much, spend too recklessly, laugh too little, drive too fast, get too angry, stay up too late, get up too tired, read too little, watch TV too much, and pray too seldom. We have multiplied our possessions, but reduced our values. We talk too much, love too seldom, and hate too often. We've learned how to make a living, but not a life. We've added years to life not life to years.

We've been all the way to the moon and back, but have trouble crossing the street to meet a new neighbor. We conquered outer space but not inner space. We've done larger things, but not better things.

We've cleaned up the air, but polluted the soul. We've conquered the atom, but not our prejudice. We write more, but learn less. We plan more, but accomplish less. We've learned to rush, but not to wait. We build more computers to hold more information, to produce more copies than ever, but we communicate less and less. These are the times of fast foods and slow digestion, big men and small character, steep profits and shallow relationships. These are the days of two incomes but more divorce, fancier houses, but broken homes. These are days of quick trips, disposable diapers, throw away morality, one night stands, overweight bodies, and pills that do everything from cheer, to quiet, to kill. It is a time when there is much in the showroom window and nothing in the stockroom. A time when technology can bring this letter to you, and a time when you can choose either to share this insight, or to just hit delete. Remember, spend some time with your loved ones, because they are not going to be around forever. Remember, say a kind word to someone who looks up to you in awe, because that little person soon will grow up and leave your side. Remember, to give a warm hug to the one next to you, because that is the only treasure you can give with your heart and it doesn't cost a cent. Remember, to say, "I love you" to your partner and your loved ones, but most of all mean it. A kiss and an embrace will mend hurt when it comes from deep inside of you. Remember to hold hands and cherish the moment for someday that person will not be there again. Give time to love, give time to speak, and give time to share the precious thoughts in your mind. Life is not measured by the number of breaths we take, but by the moments that take our breath away.

How To Stay Young
(more by George Carlin)

1. Throw out nonessential numbers. This includes age, weight and height. Let the doctor worry about them. That is why you pay him/her.

2. Keep only cheerful friends. The grouches pull you down.

3. Keep learning. Learn more about the computer, crafts, gardening, whatever. Never let the brain idle. "An idle mind is the devil's workshop." And the devil's name is Alzheimer's.

4. Enjoy the simple things.

5. Laugh often, long and loud. Laugh until you gasp for breath.

6. The tears happen. Endure, grieve, and move on. The only person who is with us our entire life, is ourselves. Be ALIVE while you are alive.

7. Surround yourself with what you love, whether it's family, pets, keepsakes, music, plants, hobbies, what ever. Your home is your refuge.

8. Cherish your health: If it is good, preserve it. If it is unstable, improve it. If it is beyond what you can improve, get help.

9. Don't take guilt trips. Take a trip to the mall, to the next county, to a foreign country, but NOT to where the guilt is.

10. Tell the people you love that you love them, at every opportunity.

"What can you do to promote world peace? Go home and love your family."

- Mother Teresa

Lexiophiles (Lovers of Words)

1. A bicycle can't stand alone because it is two-tired.

2. What's the definition of a will? It's a dead giveaway.

3. Time flies like an arrow. Fruit flies like a banana.

4. A backward poet writes inverse.

5. In democracy it's your vote that counts; In feudalism it's your count that votes.

7. A chicken crossing the road is poultry in motion.

8. If you don't pay your exorcist you get repossessed.

9. With her marriage she got a new name and a dress.

10. Show me a piano falling down a mineshaft and I'll show you A-flat minor.

11. When a clock is hungry it goes back four seconds.

12. The man who fell into an upholstery machine is fully recovered.

13. A grenade thrown into a kitchen in France would result in Linoleum Blown apart.

14. You feel stuck with your debt if you can't budge it.

15. Local Area Network in Australia: the LAN down under.

16. He often broke into song because he couldn't find the key.

17. Every calendar's days are numbered.

18. A lot of money is tainted. 'Taint yours and 'taint mine.'

19. A boiled egg in the morning is hard to beat

20. He had a photographic memory which was never developed.

21. A plateau is a high form of flattery.

22. The short fortune-teller who escaped from prison was a small medium at large.

23. Those who get too big for their britches will be exposed in the end.

24. When you've seen one shopping center you've seen a mall.

25. Those who jump off a Paris bridge are in Seine.

26. When an actress saw her first strands of gray hair, she thought she'd dye.

27. Bakers trade bread recipes on a knead to know basis.

28. Santa's helpers are subordinate clauses.

29. Acupuncture is a jab well done.

30. Marathon runners with bad footwear suffer the agony of defeat.

"If your children look up to you, you've made a success of life's biggest job."

-Anonymous

Success

At age 4 success is . . . not peeing in your pants.

At age 12 success is . . . having friends.

At age 16 success is . . . having a drivers license.

At age 20 success is . . . having sex.

At age 35 success is . . . having money.

At age 50 success is . . . having money.

At age 60 success is . . . having sex.

At age 70 success is . . . having a drivers license.

At age 75 success is . . . having friends.

At age 80 success is . . . not peeing in your pants.

Remember This One?

"The child whispered, 'God, speak to me'
And a meadow lark sang.
The child did not hear.
So the child yelled, 'God, speak to me!'
And the thunder rolled across the sky
But the child did not listen.
The child looked around and said,
'God let me see you' and a star shone brightly
But the child did not notice.
And the child shouted,
'God show me a miracle!'
And a life was born but the child did not know.
So the child cried out in despair,
'Touch me God, and let me know you are here!'
Whereupon God reached down
And touched the child.
But the child brushed the butterfly away
And walked away unknowingly."

Great Truths about Growing Old

1) Growing up is mandatory; growing old is optional.

2) Forget the health food. I need all the preservatives I can get.

3) When you fall down, you wonder what else you can do while you're down there.

4) You're getting old when you get the same sensation from a rocking chair that you once got from a roller coaster.

5) It's frustrating when you know all the answers but nobody bothers to ask you the questions.

6) Time may be a great healer, but it's a lousy beautician.

7) Wisdom comes with age, but sometimes age comes alone.

The Four States of Life

1) You believe in Santa Claus.

2) You don't believe in Santa Claus.

3) You are Santa Claus.

4) You look like Santa Claus.

Great Truths That Adults Have Learned

1) Raising teenagers is like nailing Jell-O to a tree.

2) Wrinkles don't hurt.

3) Families are like fudge…mostly sweet, with a few nuts.

4) Today's mighty oak is just yesterday's nut that hit the ground.

5) Laughing is good exercise. It's like jogging on the inside.

6) Middle age is when you choose your cereal for the fiber, not the toy.

"The Class Of 2006"

With college about to begin a new year, we were wondering about the "mind-set" of this year's incoming freshmen. Here's this year's list:

The people staring college this fall across the nation were born in 1988.

They have no meaningful recollection of the Reagan Era and probably did not know he had ever been shot.

They were prepubescent when the Persian Gulf War was waged.

There has been only one Pope in their lifetime, until last year.

They were 16 when the Soviet Union broke apart and do not remember the Cold War.

They are too young to remember the Space Shuttle blowing up.

Tiananmen Square means nothing to them.

Bottle caps have always been screw off and plastic.

Atari predates them, as do vinyl albums.

The statement "you sound like a broken record" means nothing to them.

They have never owned a record player.

They have likely never played Pac Man and have never heard of Pong.

The may have never heard of an 8 track. Compact Discs were introduced while they were still babies.

They have always had an answering machine.

Most have never seen a TV with only 13 channels, nor have they seen a black and white TV.

They have always had cable.

There have always been VCRs, but they have no idea what BETA was.

They cannot fathom not having a remote control

The don't know what a cloth baby diaper is, or know about the "Help me, I've fallen and I can't get up" commercial…. Feeling old yet? There's more:

They were born in the year that Walkman were introduced by Sony.

Roller skating has always meant inline for them.

Michael Jackson has always been white.

Jay Leno has always been on the Tonight Show. They never took a swim and thought about Jaws.

The Vietnam War is as ancient history to them as W.W.I, W.W.II and the Civil War.

They have no idea that Americans were ever held hostage in Iran.

They don't know who Mork was or where he was from (The correct answer, by the way is Ork).

They never heard: "Where's the beef?", "I'd walk a mile for a Camel", or "De plane, de plane!"

They do not care who shot J.R. and have no idea who J.R. was.

Kansas, Chicago, Boston, America and Alabama are places, not bands.

There has always been MTV.

They don't have a clue how to use a typewriter.

The Year 1906

One Hundred Years Ago.

What a difference a century makes...

Here are some statistics for the Year 1906:

The average life expectancy was 47 years.

Only 14 percent of the homes had a bathtub.

Only 8 percent of homes had a telephone.

There were only 8,000 cars and only

144 miles of paved roads.

The maximum speed limit in most cities was 10 mph.

The tallest structure in the world was the Eiffel Tower!

The average wage in 1906 was 22 cents per hour.

The average worker made between $200 and $400 per year.

A competent accountant could expect to earn
$2000 per year, and dentist $2,500 per year, a
veterinarian between $1,500 and $4,000 per year,
and a mechanical engineer about $5,000 per year.

More than 95 percent of all births were at HOME.

Ninety percent of all doctors had NO COLLEGE EDUCATION! Instead they attended so-called medical schools, many of which were condemned in the press AND the government as "substandard."

Sugar cost four cents a pound.
Eggs were fourteen cents a dozen.

In Honor of Rodney Dangerfield

(His 21 Best One Liners)

I was so poor growing up… if I wasn't a boy…I'd have had nothing to play with.

A girl phoned the other day and said, "come on over; nobody's home." I went over.
Nobody was home.

During sex my girlfriend always wants to talk to me. Just the other night she called me from a hotel.

One day I came home early from work…I say a guy jogging naked. I said to the guy, "Hey buddy, why are you doing that?" He said, "Because you came home early".

It has been a rough day. I got up this morning…put a shirt on and a button fell off. I picked up my briefcase, and the handle fell off. I'm afraid to go to the bathroom.

I was such an ugly kid…When I played in the sandbox; the cat kept covering me up.

I could tell my parents hated me. My bath toys were a toaster and a radio.

I was such an ugly baby...My mother never breast-fed me. She told me that she only liked me as a friend.

I'm so ugly...My father carried around a picture of the kid who came with the wallet.

When I was born, the doctor came into the waiting room and said to my father, "I'm sorry. We did everything we could, but he pulled through."

I'm so ugly...My mother had morning sickness... AFTER I was born.

I remember the time that I was kidnaped and they sent a piece of my finger to my father. He said he wanted more proof.

Once when I was lost, I saw a policeman, and asked him to help me find my parents. I said to him, "So you think we'll ever find them?" He said, "I don't know kid. There's so many places they can hide."

My wife made me join a bridge club. I jump off next Tuesday.

I'm so ugly...I worked in a pet shop, and the people kept asking how big I'd get.

My wife went to see my doctor. "Doctor, every morning when I get up and look in the mirror...I feel like throwing up. What's wrong with me? He said..."I don't know but your eyesight is perfect."

I went to the doctor because I'd swallowed a bottle of sleeping bills. My doctor told me to have a few drinks and get some rest.

Some dog I got. We call him Egypt because in every room he leaves a pyramid. His favorite bone is in my arm. Last night he went on the paper four times - three of those times I was reading it.

One year they wanted to make me poster boy - for birth control.

My uncle's dying wish was to have me sitting in his lap; he was in the electric chair.

The Late, Great Henny Youngman Said:

I've been in love with the same woman for 49 years. If my wife ever finds out, she'll kill me!

My wife and I have the secret to making a marriage last. Two times a week, we go to a nice restaurant, a little wine, good food…..She goes Tuesdays, I go Fridays.

Someone stole all my credit cards, but I won't be reporting it. The thief spends less than my wife did.

I take my wife everywhere, but she keeps finding her way back.

We always hold hands. If I let go, she shops.

My wife and I went back to the hotel where we spent our wedding night. Only this time, I stayed in the bathroom and cried.

She was at the beauty shop for two hours. That was only for the estimate. She got a mud pack and looked great for two days. Then the mud fell off.

I was just in London - there is a 6-hour time difference. I'm still confused. When I go to dinner, I feel sexy. When I go to bed, I feel hungry.

The doctor gave a man six months to live. The man couldn't pay his bill, so he gave him another six months.

The Doctor called Mrs. Cohen saying "Mrs. Cohen, your check came back." Mrs. Cohen answered "So did my arthritis!" The Doctor says: "You'll live to be 60!" "I AM 60!" "See, what did I tell you?"

A doctor has a stethoscope up to a man's chest. The man asks "Doc, how do I stand? "The doctor says "That's what puzzles me!"

"Doctor, I have a ringing in my ears." "Don't answer!"

A drunk was in front of a judge. The judge says "You've been brought here for drinking. The drunk says "Okay, let's get started."

The other day I broke 70. That's a lot of clubs.

I made a movie with Farrah Fawcett, and her dressing room was next to mine. There was a little hole in the wall. I let her look.

A bum asked me "Give me $10 till payday." I asked "When's payday? He said "I don't know, you're the one who is working!"

A bum came up to me saying "I haven't eaten in two days! I said, "You should force yourself!"

Another bum told me "I haven't tasted food all week. I told him "Don't worry, it still tastes the same!"

I have a lovely room and bath in the hotel. It's a little inconvenient. They're in two separate buildings!

My hotel room is so small, the mice are hunchbacked.

She's been married so many times she has rice marks on her face.

Why do Jewish divorces cost so much? They're worth it.

Why do Jewish men die before their wives? They want to.

A car hit a Jewish man. The paramedic says, "Are you comfortable? "The man says, "I make a good living."

A guy complains of a headache. Another guy says "Do what I do. I put my head on my wife's bosom,; and the headache goes away." The next day, the man says, "Did you do what I told you to?" "Yes, I sure did. By the way, you have a nice house!"

In a blackout, a Polish man was stuck on an escalator for two hours. I asked him "Why didn't you walk down?" He said, "because I was going up!"

I just got back from a pleasure trip. I took my mother-in-law to the airport.

I wish my brother would learn a trade, so I would know what kind of work he's out of.

Natural Highs

Falling in love.

Laughing so hard your face hurts.

A special glance.

Getting mail.

Taking a drive on a pretty road.

Hearing your favorite song on the radio.

Lying in bed listening to the rain outside.

Hot towels out of the dryer.

Walking out of last final.

A long distance phone call.

A good conversation.

The beach.

Finding a $20 bill in your coat from last winter.

Laughing at yourself.

Midnight phone calls that last for hours.

Running through sprinklers.

Laughing for absolutely no reason at all.

Having someone tell you that you're beautiful.

Laughing at an inside joke.

Friends.

Accidently overhearing someone say something nice about you.

Your first kiss.

Being part of a team.

Making new friends or spending time with old ones.

Late night talks with your roommate that keep you from sleeping.

Sweet dreams.

Hot chocolate.

Road trips with friends.

Swinging on swings.

Watching a good movie cuddled up on a couch with someone you love.

Song lyrics printed inside your CD so you can sing along without feeling stupid.

Getting butterflies in your stomach every time you see that one person.

Winning a really competitive game.

Making chocolate chip cookies.

Having your friends send you homemade cookies.

Spending time with close friends.

Running through the fountains with your friends.

Riding a bike downhill.

The feeling after running a few miles - an accomplishment!

Seeing smiles and hearing laughter from your friends.

Holding hands with someone you care about.

Running into an old friend and realizing that some things (good or bad) never change.

Discovering that love is unconditional and stronger than time.

Riding the best roller coasters over and over.

Hugging the person you love.

Watching the expression on someone's face as they open a much-desired present from you.

Watching the sunrise.

Getting out of bed every morning and thanking God for another beautiful day.

Vincent Van Gogh

Van Gogh had many relatives. Among them were:

His obnoxious brother, Please Gogh

His dizzy aunt, Verti Gogh

The brother who ate prunes, Gotta Gogh

The brother who worked at a convenience store, Stop n' Gogh

The grandfather from Yugoslavia, U Gogh

The brother who bleached his clothes white, Hue Gogh

The cousin from Illinois, Chica Gogh

His magician uncle, Where diddy Gogh

His Mexican cousin, Amee Gogh

The Mexican cousin's half American brother, Grin Gogh

The nephew who drove a stage coach, Wellsfar Gogh

The constipated uncle, Cant Gogh

The ballroom dancing aunt, Tan Gogh

The bird lover uncle, Flamin Gogh

His nephew psychoanalyst, E Gogh

The fruit loving cousin, Man Gogh

An aunt who taught positive thinking, Wayto Gogh

The bouncy nephew, Poe Gogh,

A sister who loved disco, Go Gogh

His Italian uncle, Day Gogh

And his niece who travels the country in a van,
Winnie Bay Gogh

"Love is not finding someone to live with, It's finding someone you can't live without."

-Anonymous

Clap and Cheer!

Whenever I'm disappointed with my spot in life, I stop and think about little Jamie Scott.

Jamie was trying out for a part in a school play. His mother told me that he'd set his heart on
being in it, though she feared he would not be chosen. On the day the parts were awarded, I went
with her to collect him after school. Jamie rushed up to her, eyes shining with pride and
excitement. "Guess what Mum," he shouted, and then said those words that will remain with me
for ever: "I've been chosen to clap and cheer!"

If I Had My Life To Live Over
by Erma Bombeck

I would have talked less and listened more...

I would have invited friends over to dinner even if,
the carpet was stained and the sofa faded...

I would have eaten the popcorn in the "GOOD"
living room and worried much less about the dirt when
someone wanted to light a fire in the fireplace...

I would have taken the time to listen to my
grandfather ramble about his youth...

I would never have insisted the car windows be
rolled up on a summer day because my hair had just
been teased and sprayed...

I would have burned the pink candle sculpted like a
rose before it melted in storage...

I would have sat on the lawn with my children and
not worried about grass stains...

I would have cried and laughed less while watching
television and more while watching life...

I would have gone to bed when I was sick instead of
pretending the earth would go into a holding pattern
if I weren't there for the day...

I would never have bought anything just because it
was practical, wouldn't show soil or was guaranteed
to last a lifetime...

Instead of wishing away nine months of pregnancy,

I'd have cherished every moment realizing that the wonderment growing inside me was the only chance in life to assist God in a miracle...

When my kids kissed me impetuously, I would never have said, "Later. Now go get washed up for dinner."

There would have been more "I love yous" ... more

"I'm sorrys" ... but mostly, given another shot at life, I would seize every minute...look at it and really see it ... live it ... and never give it back...

Ben Stein's Last Column…

How Can Someone Who Lives in Insane Luxury Be a Star in Today's World? As I begin to write this, I "slug" it, as we writers say, which means I put a heading on top of the document to identify it. This heading is "eonline FINAL," and it gives me a shiver to write it. I have been doing this column for so long that I cannot even recall when I started. I loved writing this column so much for so long I came to believe it would never end. It worked well for a long time, but gradually, my changing as a person and the world's change have overtaken it. On a small scale, Morton's, while better than ever, no longer attracts as many stars as it used to. It still brings in the rich people in droves and definitely some stars. I saw Samuel L. Jackson there a few days ago, and we had a nice visit, and right before that, I saw and had a splendid talk with Warren Beatty in an elevator, in which we agreed that Splendor in the Grass was a super movie. But Morton's is not the star galaxy it once was, though it probably will be again.

Beyond that, a bigger change has happened. I no longer think Hollywood stars are terribly important. They are uniformly pleasant, friendly people, and they treat me better than I deserve to be treated. But a man or woman who makes a huge wage for memorizing lines and reciting them in front of a camera is no longer my idea of a shining star we should all look up to. How can a man or woman who makes an eight-figure wage and lives in insane luxury really be a star in today's world, if by a "star" we mean someone bright and powerful and attractive as a role model? Real stars are not riding around in the backs of limousines or in Porsches or getting trained in yoga or Pilates and eating only raw fruit while they have Vietnamese girls do their nails. They can be interesting, nice people, but they are not heroes to me any longer. A real star is the soldier of the 4th Infantry Division who poked his head into a hole on a farm near Tikrit, Iraq. He could have been met by a bomb or a hail of AK-47 bullets. Instead, he faced an abject Saddam Hussein and the gratitude of all of the decent people of the world. A real star is the U.S. soldier who was sent to disarm a bomb next to a road north of Baghdad. He approached it, and the bomb went off and killed him. A real star, the kind who haunts my memory night and day, is the U.S. soldier in Baghdad who saw a little girl playing with a piece of unexploded ordnance on a street near where he was guarding a station. He pushed her aside and threw himself on it just as it exploded. He left a family desolate in California and a little girl alive in Baghdad. The stars who deserve media attention are not the ones who have lavish weddings on TV but the ones who patrol the streets of Mosul even after two of their buddies were murdered and their bodies battered and stripped for the sin of trying to protect Iraqis from terrorists. We put couples with incomes of $100 million a year on the covers of our magazines. The noncoms and officers who barely scrape by on military pay but stand on guard in Afghanistan and Iraq and on ships and in submarines and near the Arctic Circle are anonymous as they live and die. I am no longer comfortable being a part of the system that has such poor values, and I do not want to perpetuate those values by pretending that who is eating at Morton's is a big subject. There are plenty of other stars in the American firmament...the policemen and women who go off on patrol in South Central and have no idea if they will return alive; the orderlies and paramedics who bring in people who have been in terrible accidents and prepare them for surgery; the teachers and nurses who throw their whole spirits into caring for autistic children; the kind men and women who work in hospices and in cancer wards. Think of each and every fireman who was running up the stairs at the World Trade Center as the towers began to collapse. Now you have my idea of a real hero. I came to realize that life lived to help others is the only one that matters. This is my highest and best use as a human. I can put it another way. Years ago, I realized I could never be as great an actor as Olivier or as good a comic as Steve Martin…or Martin Mull or Fred Willard—or as good an economist as Samuelson or Friedman or as good a writer as Fitzgerald. Or even remotely close to any of them. But I could be a devoted father to my son, husband to my wife and, above all, a good son to the parents who had done so much for me. This came to be my main task in life. I did it moderately well with my son, pretty well with my wife and well indeed with my parents (with my sister's help). I cared for and paid attention to them in their declining years. I stayed with my father as he got sick, went into extremis and then into a coma and then entered immortality with my sister and me reading him the Psalms. This was the only point at which my life touched the lives of the soldiers in Iraq or the firefighters in New York. I came to realize that life lived to help others is the only one that matters and that it is my duty, in return for the lavish life God has devolved upon me, to help others He has placed in my path. This is my highest and best use as a human. Faith is not believing that God can. It is knowing that God will.

Apples and Wine

Women are like apples on trees. The best ones are at the top of the tree. Most men don't want to reach for the good ones because they are afraid of falling and getting hurt. Instead, they sometimes take the apples from the ground that aren't as good, but easy. The apples at the top think something is wrong with them, when in reality, they're amazing. They just have to wait for the right man to come along, the one who is brave enough to climb all the way to the top of the tree. Share this with women who are good apples, even those who have already been picked!

Now Men.... Men are like a fine wine. They begin as grapes, and it's up to women to stomp the crap out of them until they turn into something acceptable to have dinner with.

Analysis

1. If you're too open-minded, your brains will fall out.

2. Don't worry about what people think, they don't do it very often.

3. Going to church doesn't make you a Christian any more than standing in a garage makes you a car.

4. Artificial intelligence is no match for natural stupidity.

5. If you must choose between two evils, pick the one you've never tried before.

6. My idea of housework is to sweep the room with a glance.

7. Not one shred of evidence supports the notion that life is serious.

8. It is easier to get forgiveness than permission.

9. For every action, there is an equal and opposite government program.

10. If you look like your passport picture, you probably need the trip.

11. Bills travel through the mail at twice the speed of checks.

12. A conscience is what hurts when all of your other parts feel so good.

13. Eat well, stay fit, die anyway.

14. Men are from earth. Women are from earth. Deal with it!

15. No man has ever been shot while doing the dishes.

16. A balanced diet is a cookie in each hand.

17. Middle age is when broadness of the mind and narrowness of the waist change places.

18. Opportunities always look bigger going than coming.

19. Junk is something you've kept for years and throw away three weeks before you need it.

20. There is always one more imbecile than you counted on.

21. Experience is a wonderful thing. It enables you to recognize a mistake when you make it again.

22. By the time you can make ends meet, they move the ends.

23. Thou shall not weigh more than thy refrigerator.

24. Someone who thinks logically provides a nice contrast to the real world.

25. It ain't the jeans that make your butt look fat.

AGING IS NOT FOR SISSIES

I feel like my body has gotten totally out of shape, so I got my doctor's permission to join a fitness club and start exercising. I decided to take an aerobics class for seniors. I bent, twisted, gyrated, jumped up and down, and perspired for an hour. But, by the time I got my leotards on, the class was over. —- Reporters interviewing a 104-year-old woman: "And what do you think is the best thing about being 104?" the reporter asked. She simply replied, "No peer pressure." —- The nice thing about being senile is you can hide your own Easter eggs. —- Just before the funeral services, the undertaker came up to the very elderly widow and asked, "How old was your husband?" "98," she replied. "Two years older than me." "So you're 96," the undertaker commented. She responded, "Hardly worth going home, is it? —- I've sure gotten old! I've had two bypass surgeries, a hip replacement, new knees. Fought prostate cancer and diabetes. I'm half blind, can't hear anything quieter than a jet engine, take 40 different medications that make me dizzy, winded, and subject to blackouts. Have bouts with dementia. Have poor circulation; hardly feel my hands and feet anymore. Can't remember if I'm 85 or 92. Have lost all my friends. But, thank God, I still have my driver's license. —- A 97-year-old man goes into his doctor's office and says, "Doc, I want my sex drive lowered." "Sir," replied the doctor,"you're 97. Don't you think your sex drive is all in your head?" "You're damned right it is!" replied the old man. "That's why I want it lowered!" —- An elderly woman decided to prepare her will and told her preacher she had two final requests. First, she wanted to be cremated, and second, she wanted her ashes scattered over Wal-Mart. "Wal-Mart?" the preacher exclaimed. "Why Wal-Mart?" "Then I'll be sure my daughters visit me twice a week." —-My memory's not as sharp as it used to be. Also, my memory's not as sharp as it used to be. —- Know how to prevent sagging? Just eat till the wrinkles fill out. —-I've still got it, but nobody wants to see it. —-I'm getting into swing dancing. Not on purpose. Some parts of my body are just prone to swinging. —-It's scary when you start making the same noises as your coffee maker. —-The good news is that even as we get older, guys still look at our boobs. The bad news is they have to squat down first.

—-These days about half the stuff in my shopping cart says, "For fast relief." —-I've tried to find a suitable exercise video for women my age, but they haven't made one called "Buns of Putty." —-Don't think of it as getting hot flashes. Think of it as your inner child playing with matches. —-Don't let aging get you down. It's too hard to get back up! —- Remember: You don't stop laughing because you grow old, You grow old because you stop laughing.—THE SENILITY PRAYER: Grant me the senility to forget the people I never liked anyway, the good fortune to run into the ones I do, and the eyesight to tell the difference.

Rearrangements

DORMITORY:
When you rearrange the letters:
DIRTY ROOM

GEORGE BUSH:
When you rearrange the letters:
HE BUGS GORE

MORSE CODE:
When you rearrange the letters:
HERE COMES DOTS

SLOT MACHINES:
When you rearrange the letters:
CASH LOST IN ME

MR. MOJO RISIN'
When you rearrange the letters:
JIM MORRISON
(from the Doors song "L.A. Woman")

SNOOZE ALARMS:
When you rearrange the letters:
ALAS! NO MORE Z'S

A DECIMAL POINT:

When you rearrange the letters:

I'M A DOT IN PLACE

ELEVEN PLUS TWO:

When you rearrange the letters:

TWELVE PLUS ONE

DEBIT CARD:

When you rearrange the letters:

BAD CREDIT

ELVIS:

When you rearrange the letters:

LIVES.

Can You Relate???

1975:   Long hair
2005:   Longing for hair

1975:   KEG
2005:   EKG

1975:   Acid rock
2005:   Acid reflux

1975:   Moving to California because it's cool
2005:   Moving to California because it's warm

1975:   Trying to look like Marlon Brando or Liz Taylor
2005:   Trying NOT to look like Marlon Brando or Liz Taylor

1975:   Seeds and stems
2005:   Roughage

1975:   Hoping for BMW
2005:   Hoping for BM

1975:   The Greatful Dead
2005:   Dr. Kevorkian

1975:   Going to a new, hip joint

2005:	Receiving a new hip joint

1975:	Rolling stones
2005:	Kidney stones

1975:	Being called into the principal's office
2005:	Calling the principal's office

1975:	Screw the system
2005:	Upgrade the system

1975:	Disco
2005:	Costco

1975:	Parents begging you to get your hair cut
2005:	Children begging you to get their heads shaved

1975:	Passing the driver's test
2005:	Passing the vision test

1975:	Whatever
2005:	Depends

Mensa Invitational

1. Intaxication: Euphoria at getting a tax refund, which lasts until you realize it was your money to start with.

2. Reintarnation: Coming back to life as a hillbilly.

3. Bozone (n.): The substance surrounding stupid people that stops bright ideas from penetrating. The bozone layer, unfortunately, shows little sign of breaking down in the near future.

4. Foreploy: Any misrepresentation about yourself for the purpose of getting laid.

5. Cashtration (n.): The act of buying a house, which renders the subject financially impotent for an indefinite period.

6. Giraffiti: Vandalism spray-painted very, very high.

7. Sarchasm: The gulf between the author of sarcastic wit & the person who doesn't get it.

8. Inoculatte: To take coffee intravenously when you are running late.

9. Hipatitis: Terminal coolness.

10. Osteopornosis: A degenerate disease.

11. Karmageddon: It's like, when everybody is sending off all these really bad vibes, right? And then, like, the Earth explodes & it's like, a serious bummer.

12. Decafalon (n.): The grueling event of getting thru the day consuming only things that are good for you.

13. Glibido: All talk & no action.

14. Dopeler effect: The tendency of stupid ideas to seem smarter when they come at you rapidly.

15. Arachnoleptic fit (n.): The frantic dance performed just after you've accidentally walked thru a spider web.

16. Beelzebug (n.): Satan in the form of a mosquito, that gets into your bedroom at three in the morning & cannot be cast out.

17. Caterpallor (n.): The color you turn after finding half a worm in the fruit you're eating.

18. Ignoranus: A person who's both stupid & an asshole.

George Carlin Strikes Again…

Ever wonder about those people who spend $2.00 apiece on those little bottles of Evian water: Try spelling Evian backwards: NAIVE.

Isn't making a smoking section in a restaurant like making a peeing section in a swimming pool?

OK…so the Jacksonville Jaguars are known as the "Jags" and the Tampa Bay Buccaneers are known as the "Bucs", what does that make the Tennessee Titans?

If 4 out of 5 people SUFFER from diarrhea…does that mean that one enjoys it?

There are three religious truths:

1) Jews do not recognize Jesus as the Messiah.

2) Protestants do not recognize the Pope as the leader of the Christian faith.

3) Baptists do not recognize each other at the liquor store or at Hooters.

1. If you take an Oriental person and spin him around several times, does he become disoriented?

2. If people from Poland are called Poles, why aren't people from Holland called Holes?

3. Why do we say something is out of whack? What's a whack?

4. Do infants enjoy infancy as much as adults enjoy adultery?

5. If a pig loses its voice, is it disgruntled?

6. If love is blind, why is lingerie so popular?

7. When someone asks you. "A penny for your thoughts" and you put your two cents in...

what happens to the other penny?

8. Why is the man who invests all your money called a broker?

9. Why do crotons come in an airtight package: Aren't they just stale to begin with?

10. When cheese gets its picture taken, what does it say?

11. Why is a person who plays the piano call a pianist but a person who drives a race car not called a racist?

12. Why are a wise man and a wise guy opposites?

13. Why do overlook and oversee mean opposite things?

14. Why isn't the number 11, pronounced onety one?

15. "I am" is reportedly the shortest sentence in the English language. Could it be that "I do" is the longest sentence?

16. If lawyers are disbarred and clergymen defrocked, doesn't it follow that electricians can be delighted, musicians denoted, cowboys deranged, models deposed, tree surgeons debarked, and dry cleaners depressed?

17. IF Fed Ex and UPS were to merge, would they call it Fed UP?

18. Do Lipton Tea employees take coffee breaks?

19. What hair color do they put in the driver's licenses of bald men?

20. I was thinking about how people seem to read the Bible a whole lot more as they get older; then it dawned on me…They're cramming for their final exam.

21. I thought about how mothers feed their babies with tiny little spoons and forks, so I wondered what do Chinese mothers use … Toothpicks?

22. Why do they put pictures of criminals up in the Post Office? What are we suppose to do, write to them? Why don't they just put their pictures on postage stamps so the mailmen can look for them while they deliver the mail?

23. If it's true that we are here to help others, then what exactly are the others here for?

24. You never really learn to swear until you learn to drive.

25. No one ever says, "It's only a game" when their team is winning.

26. Ever wonder what the speed of lightening would be if it didn't zigzag?

27. Last night I played a blank tape full blast. The mime next door went nuts.

28. If a cow laughed, would milk come out of her nose?

29. Whatever happened to Preparations A through G?

Doilies

There was once a man and woman who had been married for more that 60 years. They had shared everything. They had talked about everything. Nothing was held back. Well,...almost nothing. They had kept no secrets from each other except that the little old woman had a shoe box in the top of her closet that she had cautioned her husband never to open or ask her about. For all of these years, he had never thought about the box, but one day the little old woman got very sick and the doctor said she should not recover. In trying to sort out their assets, the old man took down the shoe box and took it to his wife's bedside. She agreed that it was time that he should know what was in the box. When he opened it, he found two crocheted doilies and a stack of money totaling $250,000. Holy Moley! He asked her about the contents. "When we were to be married," she started, "my grandmother told me the secret of a happy marriage was to never argue. She told me that if I ever got angry with you, I should just keep quiet and crochet a doily." The old man was so moved, he had to fight back tears. Only two precious doilies were inside the box! She had only been angry with him two times in all those years of living and loving. He almost burst with happiness. "Honey," he said, "that explains the doilies, but...what about all this money? Where did it all come from?" "Oh," she said, "that's the money I made from selling the doilies."

For Those Who Know Everything II

The liquid inside young coconuts can be used as a substitute for Blood plasma. No piece of paper can be folded in half more than seven (7) times. Donkeys kill more people annually than plane crashes. You burn more calories sleeping than you do watching television. Oak trees do not produce acorns until they are fifty (50) years of age or older. The first product to have a bar code was Wrigley's gum. The King of Hearts is the only king WITHOUT A MOUSTACHE. American Airlines saved $40,000 in 1987 by eliminating one (1) olive from each salad served in first-class. Venus is the only planet that rotates clockwise. Apples, not caffeine, are more efficient awakening you up in the morning. Most dust particles in your house are made from DEAD SKIN!

The first owner of the Marlboro Company died of lung cancer. So did the first "Marlboro Man." Walt Disney was afraid OF MICE! PEARLS MELT IN VINEGAR! The three most valuable brand names on earth: Marlboro, Coca Cola, and Budweiser, in that order. It is possible to lead a cow upstairs... but, not downstairs. A duck's quack doesn't echo, and no one knows why. Dentists have recommended that a toothbrush be kept at least six (6) feet away from a toilet to avoid airborne particles resulting from the flush. And the best for last… Turtles can breathe through their butts.

Sometimes We Just Need To Be Reminded!

A well-known speaker started off his seminar by holding up a $20.00 bill. In the room of 200, he asked, "Who would like this $20 bill?" Hands started going up. He said, "I am going to give this $20 to one of you but first, let me do this. He proceeded to crumple up the $20 dollar bill. He then asked, "Who still wants it?" Still the hands were up in the air. Well, he replied, "What if I do this?" And he dropped it on the ground and started to grind it into the floor with his shoe. He picked it up, now crumpled and dirty. "Now, who still wants it?" Still the hands went into the air. My friends, we have all learned a very valuable lesson. No matter what I did to the money, you still wanted it because it did not decrease in value. It was still worth $20. Many times in our lives, we are dropped, crumpled, and ground into the dirt by the decisions we make and the circumstances that come our way. We feel as though we are worthless. But no matter what has happened or what will happen, you will never lose your value. Dirty or clean, crumpled or finely creased, you are still priceless to those who DO LOVE you. The worth of our lives comes not in what we do or who we know, but by WHO WE ARE. You are special- Don't

EVER forget it." If you do not pass this on, you may never know the lives it touches, the hurting hearts it speaks to, or the hope that it can bring. Count your blessings, not your problems. And remember: amateurs built the ark ... professionals built the Titanic.

"The time you enjoy wasting is not wasted time."

-Bertrand Russell

This Was Written By A Man On Death Row

If you woke up this morning with more health than illness… you are blessed more than the million who will not survive the week.

If you have never experienced the danger of battle, the loneliness of imprisonment, the agony of torture, or the pangs of starvation… you are ahead of 500 million people in the world.

If you can attend a church meeting without fear of harassment, arrest, torture, or death... you are more blessed than three billion people in the world.

If you have food in the refrigerator, clothes on your back, a roof overhead and a place to sleep… you are richer than 75% of the world.

If you have money in the bank, in your wallet and spare change in a dish someplace… you are among the top 8% of the world's wealthy.

If your parents are still alive and married…you are very rare, even in the United States.

If you hold up your head with a smile on your face and are truly thankful…you are blessed because the majority can, but most do not.

If you can hold someone's hand, hug them or even touch them on the shoulder… you are blessed because you can offer God's healing touch.

If you can read this message, you just received a double blessing in that someone was thinking of you, and furthermore, you are more blessed than over two billion people in the world who cannot read at all.

"Happiness is an imaginary condition, formerly attributed by the living to the dead, now usually attributed by adults to children and by children to adults."

- Thomas Szasz,

Reasons Why The English Language Is So Hard To Learn

The bandage was wound around the wound. The farm was used to produce produce. The dump was so full that it had to refuse more refuse. We must polish the Polish furniture. He could lead if he would get the lead out. The soldier decided to desert his dessert in the desert. Since there is no time like the present, he thought it was time to present the present. A bass was painted on the head of the bass drum. When shot at, the dove dove into the bushes. I did not object to the object. The insurance was invalid for the invalid. There was a row among the oarsmen about how to row. They were too close to the door to close it. The buck does funny things when the does are present. A seamstress and a sewer fell down into a sewer line. To help with planting, the farmer taught his sow to sow. The wind was too strong to wind the sail. After a number of injections my jaw got number.

Upon seeing the tear in the painting I shed a tear. I had to subject the subject to a series of tests.

How can I intimate this to my most intimate friend? There is no egg in eggplant nor ham in hamburger; neither apple nor pine in pineapple. English muffins weren't invented in England or French fries in France.

Sweetmeats are candies while sweetbreads, which aren't sweet, are meat. Quicksand works slowly, boxing rings are square and a guinea pig is neither from Guinea nor is it a pig. And why is it that writers write, but fingers don't fing, grocers don't groce and hammers don't ham? If the plural of tooth is teeth, why isn't the plural of booth beeth? One goose, 2 geese. So one moose, 2 meese? Doesn't it seem crazy that you can make amends but not one amend. If you have a bunch of odds and ends and get rid of all but one of them, what do you call it? Is it an odd, or an end? If teachers taught, why didn't preachers praught? If a vegetarian eats vegetables, what does a humanitarian eat? In what language do people recite at a play and play at a recital? Ship by truck and send cargo by ship? Have noses that run and feet that smell? How can a slim chance and a fat chance be the same, while a wise man and a wise guy are opposites? You have to marvel at the unique lunacy of a language in which your house can burn up as it burns down, in which you fill in a form by filling it out, and in which, an alarm goes off by going on. English was invented by people, not computers, and it reflects the creativity of the human race, which, of course, is not a race at all. That is why, when the stars are out, they are visible, but when the lights are out, they are invisible. P.S. Why doesn't "Buick" rhyme with "quick"?

So You Think You Know Everything?

A dime has 118 ridges around the edge.

A cat has 32 muscles in each ear.

A crocodile cannot stick out its tongue.

A dragonfly has a life span of 24 hours.

A goldfish has a memory span of three seconds.

A "jiffy" is an actual unit of time for 1/100th of a second.

A shark is the only fish that can blink with both eyes.

A snail can sleep for three years.

Al Capone's business card said he was a used furniture dealer.

All 50 states are listed across the top of the Lincoln Memorial on the back of the $5 bill.

Almonds are a member of the peach family.

An ostrich's eye is bigger than its brain.

Babies are born without kneecaps. They don't appear until the child reaches 2 to 6 years of age.

Butterflies taste with their feet.

Cats have over one hundred vocal sounds. Dogs only have about 10.

"Dreamt" is the only English word that ends in the letters "mt".

February 1865 is the only month in recorded history that did not have a full moon.

In the last 4,000 years, no new animals have been domesticated.

If the population of China walked past you, in single file, the line would never end because of the rate of reproduction.

If you are an average American, in your whole life, you will spend an average of 6 months waiting at red lights.

It's impossible to sneeze with your eyes open.

Maine is the only state whose name is just one syllable.

No word in the English language rhymes with month, orange, silver, or purple.

On a Canadian two dollar bill, the flag flying over the Parliament building is an American flag.

Our eyes are always the same size from birth, but our nose and ears never stop growing.

Peanuts are one of the ingredients of dynamite.

Rubber bands last longer when refrigerated.

"Stewardesses" is the longest word typed with only the left hand and "lollipop" with your right.

The average person's left hand does 56% of the typing. The cruise liner, QE2, moves only six inches for each gallon of diesel that it burns.

The microwave was invented after a researcher walked by a radar tube and a chocolate bar melted in his pocket.

The sentence: "The quick brown fox jumps over the lazy dog" uses every letter of the alphabet.

The winter of 1932 was so cold that Niagara Falls froze completely solid.

The words 'race car,' 'kayak' and 'level' are the same whether they are read left to right or right to left (palindromes).

There are 293 ways to make change for a dollar.

There are more chickens than people in the world.

There are only four words in the English language which end in "dous": tremendous, horrendous, stupendous, and hazardous. There are two words in the English language that have all five vowels in order: "abstemious" and "facetious."

There's no Betty Rubble in the Flintstones Chewables Vitamins.

Tigers have striped skin, not just striped fur.

TYPEWRITER is the longest word that can be made using the letters only on one row of the keyboard.

Winston Churchill was born in a ladies' room during a dance.

Women blink nearly twice as much as men.

Your stomach has to produce a new layer of mucus every two weeks; otherwise it will digest itself.

"Daddy, How Was I Born?"

Dad says "Ah, my son, I guess one day you will need to find out anyway! Well, you see your Mom and I first got together in a chat room on MSN. Then I set up a date via e-mail with your mom and we met at a cyber-café. We sneaked into a secluded room, where your mother agreed to a download of my hard drive. As soon as I was ready to upload, we discovered that neither one of us had used a firewall, and since it was too late to hit the delete button, nine moths later a blessed little Pop-Up appeared and said: "You've got Male!"

"We could learn a lot from crayons: some are sharp, some are pretty, some are dull, some have weird names, and all are different colors... but they all exist very nicely in the same box."

-Anonymous

How The Poor Live

One day a father of a very wealthy family took his son on a trip to the country with the firm purpose of showing his son how poor people live. They spent a couple of days and nights on the farm of what would be considered a very poor family. On their return from their trip, the father asked his son, "How was the trip?" "It was great, Dad." "Did you see how poor people live?" the father asked. "Oh yes," said the son. "So, tell me, what did you learn from the trip?" asked the father. The son answered: "I saw that we have one dog and they had four. We have a pool that reaches to the middle of our garden and they have a river that has no end. We have imported lanterns in our garden and they have the stars at night. Our patio reaches to the front yard and they have the whole horizon. We have a small piece of land to live on and they have fields that go beyond our sight. We have servants who serve us, but they serve others. We buy our food, but they grow theirs. We have walls around our property to protect us, they have friends to protect them." The boy's father was speechless.

Then his son added, "Thanks, Dad, for showing me how poor we are." Isn't perspective a wonderful thing? Makes you wonder what would happen if we all gave thanks for everything we have, instead of worrying about what we don't have. Appreciate every single thing you have, especially your friends!" Life is too short and friends are too few."

To All The Kids Who Were Born In The 1930s, 40s, 50s, 60s and 70s

First, we survived being born to mothers who smoked and/or drank while they carried us. They took aspirin, ate blue cheese dressing, tuna from a can, and didn't get tested for diabetes. Then after that trauma, our baby cribs were covered with bright colored lead-based paints. We had no childproof lids on medicine bottles, doors or cabinets and when we rode our bikes, we had no helmets, not to mention, the risks we took hitchhiking. As children, we would ride in cars with no seat belts or air bags. Riding in the back of a pick up on a warm day was always a special treat. We drank water from the garden hose and NOT from a bottle. We shared one soft drink with four friends, from one bottle and NO ONE actually died from this. We ate cupcakes, white bread and real butter and drank soda pop with sugar in it, but we weren't overweight because... WE WERE ALWAYS OUTSIDE PLAYING! We would leave home in the morning and play all day, as long as we were back when the streetlights came on. No one was able to reach us all day. And we were O.K. We would spend hours building our go-carts out of scraps and then ride down the hill, only to find out we forgot the brakes. After running into the bushes a few times, we learned to solve the problem. We did not have Playstations, Nintendo's, X-boxes, no video games at all, no 99 channels on cable, no video tape movies, no surround sound, no cell phones, no personal computers, no Internet or Internet chat rooms… WE HAD FRIENDS and we went outside and found them! We fell out of trees, got cut, broke bones and teeth and there were no lawsuits from these accidents. We ate worms and mud pies made from dirt, and the worms did not live in us forever. We were given BB guns for our 10th birthdays, made up games with sticks and tennis balls and although we were told it would happen, we did not put out very many eyes. We rode bikes or walked to a friend's house and knocked on the door or rang the bell, or just yelled for them! Little League had tryouts and not everyone made the team. Those who didn't had to learn to deal with disappointment.

The idea of a parent bailing us out if we broke the law was unheard of. They actually sided with the law!

Lawyers

Lawyers should never ask a witness a question if they are not prepared for the answer. In a trial, a Southern small town prosecuting attorney called this first witness, a grand motherly, elderly woman to the stand. He approached her and asked, "Mrs. Jones, do you know me?"

She responded, "Why, yes I do know you. Mr. Williams. I have known you since you were a young boy, and frankly, you have been a big disappointment to me. You lie, you cheat on your wife, and you manipulate people and talk about them behind their backs. You think you are a big shot when you haven't got the brains to realize you never will amount to anything more than a two-bit paper pusher. Yes, I know you."

The lawyer was stunned! Not knowing what else to do, he pointed across the room and asked,

"Mrs. Jones, do you know the defense attorney?"

She again replied, "Why yes, I do. I have known Mr. Bradley since he was a youngster too.

He is lazy, bigoted, and has a drinking problem. He cannot build a normal relationship with anyone and his law practice is one of the worst in the entire state. Not to mention he cheated on his wife with three different women. One of them was your wife. Yes, I know him."

The defense attorney almost died. The judge asked both counselors to approach the bench, and in a very quiet voice, said,

"If either of you bastards asks her if she knows me, I'll throw you sorry asses in jail for contempt."

Noah in the Year 2006

In the year 2006, the Lord came unto Noah, who was now living in the United States, and said, "Once again, the earth has become wicked and over-populated and I see the end of all flesh before me. Build another Ark and save two of every living thing along with a few good humans." He gave Noah the blueprints, saying, "You have six months to build the Ark before I will start the unending rain for 40 days and 40 nights". Six months later, the Lord looked down and saw Noah weeping in his yard …. but no ark." Noah", He roared, "I'm about to start the rain! Where is the Ark?" "Forgive me, Lord," begged Noah. "But things have changed. I needed a building permit. I've been arguing with the inspector about the need for a sprinkler system. My neighbors claim that I've violated the neighborhood zoning laws by building the Ark in my yard and exceeding the height limitations. We had to go to the Development Appeal Board for a decision. Then the Department of Transportation demanded a bond be posted for the future costs of moving power lines and other overhead obstructions, to clear the passage for the Ark's move to the sea. I argued that the sea would be coming to us, but they would hear nothing of it. Getting the wood was another problem. There's a ban on cutting local trees in order to save the spotted owl. I tried to convince the environmentalists that I needed the wood to save the owls. But no go! When I started gathering the animals, I got sued by an animal rights group. They insisted that I was confining wild animals against their will. As well, they argued the accommodation was too restrictive and it was cruel and inhumane to put so many animals in a confined space. Then the EPA ruled that I couldn't build the Ark until they'd conducted an environmental impact study on your proposed flood I'm still trying to resolve a complaint with the Human Rights Commission on how many minorities I'm supposed to hire for my building crew. Also, the trades unions say I can't use my sons. They insist I have to hire only Union workers with Ark building experience. To make matters worse, the IRS seized all my assets, claiming I'm trying to leave the country illegally with endangered species. So, forgive me, Lord, but it would take at least ten years for me to finish this Ark." Suddenly the skies cleared, the sun began to shine, and a rainbow stretched across the sky. Noah looked up in wonder and asked, "You mean, You're not going to destroy the world?" "No," said the Lord. "The government beat me to it."

"I know not with what weapons
World War III will be fought,
but World War IV will be
fought with sticks and stones."

— Albert Einstein

Pun Fun

Two antennas met on a roof, fell in love and got married. The ceremony wasn't much, but the reception was excellent. A jumper cable walks into a bar. The bartender says, "I'll serve you, but don't start anything." Two peanuts walk into a bar, and one was a salted. A dyslexic man walks into a bra. A man walks into a bar with a slab of asphalt under his arm and says:"A beer please, and one for the road!" "Doc, I can't stop singing 'The Green, Green Grass of Home.'" "That sounds like Tom Jones Syndrome.""Is it common?"" Well, It's Not Unusual." Two cows are standing next to each other in a field. Daisy says to Dolly, "I was artificially inseminated this morning." "I don't believe you," says Dolly." It's true, no bull!" exclaims Daisy. An invisible man marries an invisible woman. The kids are nothing to look at either. I tried to buy some camouflage trousers the other day, but I couldn't find any. I went to a seafood disco last week... and pulled a mussel. What do you call a fish with no eyes? A fsh. Two termites walk into a bar. One asks, "Is the bar tender here?" A vulture boards an airplane, carrying two dead raccoons. The stewardess looks at him and says, "I'm sorry, sir, only one carrion allowed per passenger." Two fish swim into a concrete wall. The one turns to the other and says"Dam!". Two Eskimos sitting in a kayak were chilly, so they lit a fire in the craft. Unsurprisingly it sank, proving once again that you can't have your kayak and heat it too. Two hydrogen atoms meet. One says, "I've lost my electron." The other says, "Are you sure?" The first replies, "Yes, I'm positive."Did you hear about the Buddhist who refused Novocaine during a root canal? His goal: transcend dental medication. A group of chess enthusiasts checked into a hotel and were standing in the lobby discussing their recent tournament victories. After about an hour, the manager came out of the office and asked them to disperse. "But why?"they asked, as they moved off. "Because,"he said, "I can't stand chess-nuts boasting in an open foyer!" A woman has twins and gives them up for adoption. One of them goes to a family in Egypt and is named "Ahmal." The other goes to a family in Spain; they name him "Juan." Years later, Juan sends a picture of himself to his birth mother. Upon receiving the picture, she tells her husband that she wishes she also had a picture of Ahmal. Her husband responds,"They're twins! If you've seen Juan, you've seen Ahmal!" Mahatma Gandhi, as you know, walked barefoot most of the time, which produced an impressive set of calluses on his feet. He also ate very little, which made him rather frail—and with his odd diet, he suffered from bad breath. This made him . . . A supercalloused fragile mystic hexed by halitosis! And finally, there was the person who sent ten different puns to her friends, with the hope that at least one of the puns would make them laugh. No pun in ten did.

"I love Mickey Mouse more than any woman I've ever known."

- Walt Disney

"Mom, Why are you crying?"

"Why are you crying?" he asked his mom.

"Because I'm a woman" she told him.

I don't understand," he said.

His mom just hugged him and said,

"and you never will"…

Later the little boy asked his father "Why does mother seem to cry for no reason?"

"All women cry for no reason" was all his dad could say…

The little boy grew up and became a man, still wondering why women cry…

Finally he put in a call to GOD; when GOD got on the phone the man said, GOD, why do women cry so easily?"

GOD said…

When I made women she had to be special…

I made her shoulders strong enough to carry the weight of the world; yet, gentle enough to give comfort…

I gave her an inner strength to endure childbirth and the rejection that many times comes from her children…

I gave her a hardness that allows her to keep going when everyone else gives up and take care of her family through sickness and fatigue without complaining…

I gave her the sensitivity to love her children under any and all circumstances, even when her child has hurt them very badly...

This same sensitivity helps her to make a child's boo-boo feel better and shares in their teenagers anxieties and fears...

I gave her strength to carry her husband through his faults and fashioned her from his rib to protect his heart.

I gave her wisdom to know that a good husband never hurts his wife, but sometimes tests her strengths and her resolve to stand beside him unfalteringly.

I gave her a tear to shed, It's hers exclusively to use whenever it is needed.

It's her only weakness...It's a tear for mankind...

Murphy's Laws on Sex

The more beautiful the woman is who loves you, the easier it is to leave her with no hard feelings.

Nothing improves with age. No matter how many times you've had it, if it's offered take it, because it'll never be quite the same again.

Sex has no calories.

Sex takes up the least amount of time and causes the most amount of trouble.

There is no remedy for sex but more sex.

Sex appeal is 50% what you've got and 50% what people think you've got.

No sex with anyone in the same office.

Sex is like snow; you never know how many inches you are going to get or how long it is going to last.

A man with a house is worth two in the street.

If you get them by the balls, their hearts and minds will follow.

Virginity can be cured.

When a man's wife learns to understand him, she usually stops listening to him.

Never sleep with anyone crazier than yourself.

The qualities that most attract a woman to a man are usually the same ones she can't stand years later.

Sex is dirty only if its done right.

It is always the wrong time of the month.

The best way to hold a man is in your arms.

When the lights are out, all women are beautiful.

Sex is hereditary. If your parents never had it, chances you won't either.

"An intellectual snob is someone who can listen to the William Tell Overture and not think of The Lone Ranger."

— Dan Rather

Beware of the Holidays

In the beginning God covered the earth with broccoli and cauliflower and spinach, green and yellow and red vegetables of all kinds, so Man and Woman would live long and healthy lives. Then using God's bountiful gifts, Satan created Ben and Jerry's and Krispy Kreme. And Satan said, "You want fudge with that?" And Man said "Yes!" and Woman said, "I'll have another with sprinkles."

And lo they gained 10 pounds.

And God created healthful yogurt that Woman might keep the figure that Man found so fair. And Satan brought forth white flour from the wheat, and sugar from the cane, and combined them.

And Woman went from size 2 to size 14.

So God said, "Try my fresh green garden salad." And Satan presented crumbled bleu cheese dressing and garlic toast on the side.

And Man and Woman unfastened their belts following the repast.

God then said, "I have sent you hearty healthy vegetables and olive oil in which to cook them." And Satan brought forth deep fried coconut shrimp, butter-dipped lobster chunks and chicken-fried steak so big it needed its own platter.

And Man's cholesterol went through then roof.

God then brought forth running shoes so that his Children might lose those extra pounds.

And Satan came forth with a cable TV with remote control so Man would not have to toil changing the channels. And Man and Woman laughed and cried before the flickering light and started wearing stretch jogging suits.

Murphy's Top 10 Laws of Computing

1. When computing, whatever happens, behave as though you meant it to happen.

2. When you get to the point where you really understand your computer, it's probably obsolete.

3. The first place to look for information is the section on the manual where you'd least expect to find it.

4. When the going gets tough, upgrade.

5. For every action, there is an equal and opposite malfunction.

6. To err is human…to blame your computer for your mistakes is even more human, it's downright natural.

7. He who laughs last, probably has a back-up.

8. The number one cause of computer problems is computer solutions.

9. A complex system that doesn't work in unvariably found to have evolved from a simpler system that worked just fine.

10. A computer program will always do what you tell it to do, but rarely what you want it to do.

What Words REALLY Mean

ADULT: A person who has stopped growing at both ends and is now growing in the middle.

BEAUTY PARLOR: A place where women curl up and dye.

CANNIBAL: Someone who is fed up with people.

CHICKENS: The only animals you eat before they are born and after they are dead.

COMMITTEE: A body that keeps minutes and wastes hours.

DUST: Mud with the juice squeezed out.

EGOTIST: Someone who is usually me-deep in conversation.

HANDKERCHIEF: Cold Storage.

INFLATION: Cutting money in half without damaging the paper.

MOSQUITO: An insect that makes you like flies better.

RAISIN: Grape with a sunburn.

SECRET: Something you tell to one person at a time.

TOOTHACHE: The pain that drives you to extraction.

TOMORROW: One of the greatest labor saving devices of today.

YAWN: An honest opinion openly expressed.

WRINKLES: Something other people have. You have character lines.

"The universe is a big place,
perhaps the biggest."

- Kilgore Trout

The Five Balls

Imagine life as a game in which you are juggling some five balls in the air.

You name them - work, family, health, friends and spirit, and you are keeping all of these in the air.

You soon understand that "work" is a rubber ball. If you drop it, it will bounce back.

But the other four balls - family, health, friends and spirit - are made of glass.

If you drop one of these, they will be irrevocably scuffed, marked, nicked, damaged, or even shattered. They will never be the same. You must understand that and strive every day for balance in your life. How?

*Don't undermine your worth by comparing yourself with others. It is because we are different that each of us is special and needed. - Don't set your goals according to what other people deem important. Only you know what is best for you.

*Don't ever take for granted the things closest to your heart. Cling to them as you would your life, for without them, your life is meaningless. - Don't be afraid to encounter risks. It is only by taking chances that we learn to be brave, and succeed.

*Don't give up when you still have something to give. Nothing is ever really over until you stop trying.

*Don't shut love out of your life by saying it isn't important to find. The quickest way to find love is to give; the fastest way to lose love is to hold it too tightly; and the best way to keep love is to give it wings. - Don't be afraid to admit you are less than perfect. It is the fragile thread that binds us all together, and...

*Don't let life slip through your fingers by living in the past, or worrying about the future. BY living in the moment, one day at a time, you will live ALL the days of your live.

"Enjoy the little things in life, for one day you may look back and realize they were the big things."

-Anonymous

Things You Never Learned In Hebrew School

1.   The High Holidays have absolutely nothing to do with marijuana.

2.   Where there's smoke, there may be smoked salmon.

3.   No meal is complete without leftovers.

4.   According to Jewish dietary law, pork and shellfish may be eaten only in Chinese restaurants.

5.   A schmata is a dress that your husband's ex is wearing.

6.   You need 10 men for a minion, but only 4 in polyester pants and white shoes for pinochle.

7.   One mitzvah can change the world; two will just make you tired.

8.   After the destruction of the Second temple, God created Loehmann's.

9.   Anything worth saying is work repeating a thousand times.

10. Never take a front row seat at a bris.

11. Next year in Jerusalem. The year after that, how about a nice cruise?

12. Never leave a restaurant empty handed.

13. Spring ahead, fall back, winter in Boca Raton.

14. WASPs leave and never say good-bye; Jews say good-bye and never leave.

15. Always whisper the names of diseases.

16. If it tastes good, it's probably not kosher.

17. The important Jewish holidays are the ones on which alternate-side-of-the-street parking is suspended.

18. Without Jewish mothers, who would need therapy?

19. Before you read the menu, read the prices. If you have to ask the price, you can't afford it. But if you can afford it, make sure to tell everybody what you paid.

20. Laugh now, but one day you'll be driving a Lexus and eating dinner at four in the afternoon in Florida at the Early Bird Special.

THE BEST EMAIL OF THE YEAR!

A man was sick and tired of going to work every day while his wife stayed home. He wanted her to see what he went through so he prayed:"Dear Lord: I go to work every day and put in 8 hours while my wife merely stays at home. I want her to know what I go through, so please allow her body to switch with mine for a day. Amen. God, in his infinite wisdom, granted the man's wish. The next morning, sure enough, the man awoke as a woman.

He arose, cooked breakfast for his mate, awakened the kids, set out their school clothes, fed them breakfast, packed their lunches, drove them to school, came home and picked up the dry cleaning, took it to the cleaners and stopped at the bank to make a deposit, went grocery shopping, then drove home to put away the groceries, paid the bills and balanced the check book. He cleaned the cat's litter box and bathed the dog. Then it was already 1 P.M. and he hurried to make the beds, do the laundry, vacuum, dust, and sweep and mop the kitchen floor. Ran to the school to pick up the kids and got into an argument with them on the way home. Set out milk and cookies and got the kids organized to do their homework, then set up the ironing board and watched TV while he did the ironing. At 4:30 he began peeling potatoes and washing vegetables for salad, breaded the pork chops and snapped fresh beans for supper.

After supper, he cleaned the kitchen, ran the dishwasher, folded laundry, bathed the kids, and put them to bed. At 9 P.M. he was exhausted and, though his daily chores weren't finished, he went to bed where he was expected to make love, which he managed to get through without complaint. The next morning, he awoke and immediately knelt by the bed and said,Lord,I don't know what I was thinking. I was so wrong to envy my wife's being able to stay home all day. Please, oh please, let us trade back."The Lord, in his infinite wisdom, replied, "My son, I feel you have learned your lesson and I will be happy to change things back to the way they were. You'll just have to wait nine months, though. You got pregnant last night." Voted Women's Favorite Email of the Year.

www.ingramcontent.com/pod-product-compliance
Lightning Source LLC
Chambersburg PA
CBHW051048050326
40690CB00006B/637